ESSAYS AND STUDIES
1969

BEING VOLUME TWENTY-TWO OF THE NEW SERIES
OF ESSAYS AND STUDIES COLLECTED FOR
THE ENGLISH ASSOCIATION

BY FRANCIS BERRY

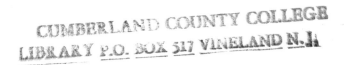
JOHN MURRAY
FIFTY ALBEMARLE STREET LONDON

© The English Association 1969

Printed in Great Britain by
Cox & Wyman Ltd, London, Fakenham and Reading
SBN 7195 1908 x

Contents

Plate

The Icelandic Sagas and their English Translators

JOHANNA TORRINGA

MUCH of the medieval prose literature of Iceland is still untranslated. Yet in the English-speaking world perhaps more efforts have been made to give the Icelandic sagas a new audience than anywhere else outside Scandinavia. For over a century there has been a steady flow of translations into English, so that by now the best and best-known specimens of Icelandic saga have found an audience on both sides of the Atlantic. The work is not finished: there is scope both for new translations and for the reappraisal of old ones. It is early days to start judging who has served the Icelandic sagas and their English readers best, but not perhaps too soon to take a look at a little of what has so far been done.

> The day after men went to the Hill of Laws. Then Hall of the Side stood up and asked for a hearing, and got it at once; and he spoke thus, 'Here there have been hard happenings in lawsuits and loss of life at the Thing, and now I will show again that I am little-hearted, for I will now ask Asgrim and the others who take the lead in these suits, that they grant us an atonement on even terms'; and so he goes on with many fair words.
>
> Kari Solmund's son said, 'Though all others take an atonement in their quarrels, yet will I take no atonement in my quarrel; for ye will wish to weigh these manslayings against the burning, and we cannot bear that.'
>
> In the same way spoke Thorgeir Craggeir.

This comes from Chapter 144 of *Njáls Saga* in the translation which Sir George Webbe Dasent completed and published in 1861 as *The Story of Burnt Njal*, and which has since 1911 been published in Everyman's Library. Below follows the corresponding passage[1] in the translation made almost a century later by Magnus Magnusson and Hermann Pálsson, (*Njal's Saga*, Penguin Classics, 1960):

> Next day everyone went to the Law Rock. Hall of Sida stood up and asked for a hearing, which was granted at once. He said, 'There have been harsh happenings here, in loss of life and lawsuits. Now I shall let it be seen that I am no hero; I want to ask Asgrim and those others who are behind these lawsuits, to grant us a settlement on even terms.' He pleaded with them eloquently and persuasively.
>
> Kari replied, 'Even though all the others accept settlements, I shall never do so. You are trying to equate the Burning with these killings, and that we could never tolerate.'
>
> Thorgeir Skorar-Geir said the same.

One notices here that the words of Latin origin replace, in the new version, their Germanic equivalents. One notices too that the paratactic constructions of the old version, in which it was possible to detect the cadences of its Icelandic original, have been broken up. But the most striking change is the one which affects the tone and atmosphere of the passage—the almost Biblical ring of Kari's reply is gone. And this is a pity, for it suited the solemnity of the moment and emphasized the momentousness of Kari's dreadful resolve to demand no payment for the death of his kinsmen except in blood.

On the whole, the passage is not long or representative enough to reveal the merits or defects of either translation. But the two versions are worth quoting side by side because, even in those few differences between the old and the new, one can discern the translators' different interpretations of their task. Vocabulary and syntax of the older version show a penchant for the romance of steadfastness and heroism, a desire also to preserve atmosphere. The new translation aims at clarity and readability— Kari's voice in the passage just quoted sounds merely business-like.

[1] Chapter 145 in this version; a third translation, by Carl F. Bayerschmidt and Lee M. Hollander (New York, 1955), has not been dealt with here.

Ideas on the duty of the translator have changed considerably during the last hundred and twenty years. When G. W. Dasent published his first translation from the Icelandic (*The Prose or Younger Edda, commonly ascribed to Snorri Sturluson*, Stockholm and London, 1842),

> . . . his chief wish was to make it as faithful as possible, and though he knows that it might have been smoother throughout, and that it contains much that will seem harsh and abrupt, both in wording and in construction, to the polished ears of the 19th century, he could not help himself in these respects, his aim being to make a translation, not a paraphrase. (Preface, pp. vi–vii)

And in the Preface to the first edition of *The Story of Burnt Njal* he wrote this:

> The duty of a translator is not to convey the sense of his original in such a way that the idioms and wording of one tongue are sacrificed to those of the other, but to find out the words and idioms of his own language which answer most fully and fairly to those of the language from which he is translating, and so to make the one as perfect a reflection as is possible of the forms and thoughts of the other. (pp. xiv–xv)

He had no intention of wooing 'the modern reader'. In this respect he differed greatly from the translators of today. He was devoted to the language of his original and, like Sir Richard Burton, he wished to give his English audience some idea of what this language was like. For him, an accurate rendering of the contents was not enough: it needed an equally faithful rendering of the spirit, the atmosphere of the saga, which he thought he could best convey by means of an imitation, in English, of its stylistic and idiomatic peculiarities. His intention was, in fact, to educate his readers to the enjoyment of something as near in flavour to the original as he could make it. Readers of today get no such education. Although whole libraries of 'world literature' are translated for their benefit, it is the policy of most translators to smooth away the alien qualities and to make even the most intractably foreign work readable and easily assimilated.

Every age discovers what it needs and most wants to find. The translators of the nineteenth century found in the prose literature of medieval Iceland tales of a rugged and remote past, made romantic by the long passage of time. In the language and style of their translations they tried to convey their impressions of the gigantic strangeness of this past, the superhuman strength of its heroes, and the magnitude of the scale on which they planned their lives of vengeance and adventure. These things were too big to be expressed in the humdrum idioms of ordinary English. William Morris used a pseudo-archaic form of English created specially for the purpose of expressing these qualities of strangeness and remoteness. Less contrived and artificial is the work of Sir George Webbe Dasent, yet his early translation shows the same tendency to bring out antique flavours by means of an English which never existed:

> Then said Gángleri; Mickle tidings cans't thou to tell of heaven, what more headseats are there than (that) at Urþr's spring? (*The Prose or Younger Edda*, p. 21)

In contrast to this are the language and style of the twentieth-century translators, who favour the homely and the colloquial to indicate that human nature has remained human nature in spite of a lapse of seven, or even ten, centuries, and that there is no new thing under the sun:

> Home he went, to tell his friend how Blund-Ketil was a paragon of men in his dealings, and how he had helped him out of the fix he was in; and this friend told his friend, and in this fashion the affair became known all over the country-side. (Gwyn Jones, 'Hen-Thorir' in *Eirik the Red and other Icelandic Sagas*, World's Classics, 1961, p. 8)

The variety of style and mood of the available English translations tends to obscure one aspect of the Icelandic sagas of which every reader should be made aware: this is their conventionality. In spite of their enormous range of subjects, the sagas are full of conventional situations and events. Readers of a family saga at once recognize such situations and incidents from their knowledge of other family sagas, recognize them not merely from their content but sometimes from their very wording.

Some, like the rides to the Thing and the Yuletide visits, the wedding feasts, the farming and the manslayings, are recurring features in the sagas because they were the common experience of all freeborn Icelanders. Slightly less frequent must have been the ships that put into Icelandic harbours from the open sea, always to be met by someone in the district who would ride to the ship to invite the captain home with him. And rarer still, resting on hearsay more often than actual experience, were the visits of Icelanders to Norwegian, Danish and English kings. Yet few Icelandic family sagas are without such events.

Traditional also are the confabulations in the open air. For these there is a formula with its variations:

> Bergthora asked Njal, 'What are they talking about out of doors?' (G. W. Dasent, *The Story of Burnt Njal*, p. 201)

> The boy went and told them that Thorir would not be coming out.
> 'Ah well,' said Blund-Ketil, 'in that case we'll be coming in.' (Gwyn Jones, 'Hen-Thorir', op. cit., p. 10)

Some of the customs and manners of the Icelanders, as they emerge again and again from the family sagas, have obviously been touched by literary convention, though it is not always easy to say how strongly it has coloured them. For instance, it is possible that women egged their reluctant menfolk on to vengeance and often flung at them the bloodstained garments of their dead kinsmen; but this is a fine dramatic gesture, which almost certainly owes more to art than life. And similarly, the sarcastic rejoinders and the famous last words may have been at least a desirable part of the brave Icelander's behaviour; but in the sagas they appear regularly as devices to suggest ruthlessness or intrepidity of character:

> Skarphedinn said, 'Hallgerda does not let our housecarles die
> of old age.' (G. W. Dasent, *The Story of Burnt Njal*, p. 68)

> 'Why is thine axe bloody?' asks Gudbrand.
> 'I made it so by doing a piece of work on thy overseer
> Asvard's back,' says Hrapp. (Ibid., p. 153)

Such is the grim humour with which the characters of Icelandic
saga approach situations of violence and disaster, even when the
disaster is their own death:

> Atli said when he received the thrust: 'They use broad
> spear-blades nowadays.'
> Then he fell forward on the threshold. The women who
> were inside came out and saw that he was dead. (G. A. Hight,
> *The Saga of Grettir the Strong*, Everyman's Library, 1965, p. 121)

Likewise conventional are the narrative formulae, less easily
detectable in translation than those recurrent themes just mentioned, unless one turns to translators like G. W. Dasent and
Muriel Press whose style and idioms remain purposely close to the
original Icelandic:

> Ingjald was the name of a man.

> The tale is told of Hrapp that he became most violent in his
> behaviour . . .

> The Thing was quiet, and not tidings to tell of it. (Muriel
> Press, *The Laxdale Saga*, Everyman's Library, 1964, pp. 29, 41
> and 189)

> Now we must take up the story, and say how Thrain Sigfus'
> son came to Norway.

> Now, the story must go back to Thorwald's mates, how there
> they are, and how they begged the loan of a boat . . .

> Now Hauskuld fares home with Kettle, and is with him some
> time.

> Now Gunnar sits at home for some time, and all is quiet.

Hogni kept up his friendship with Njal, and he is now out of the story. (G. W. Dasent, *The Story of Burnt Njal*, pp. 142, 22, 173, 124 and 142)

Now these formulae are so much part of the narrative technique of the authors that no translator ought to do away with them, however great his concern for his readers or his devotion to the virtues of 'good modern English' may be. But in the translation of *Njáls Saga* by Magnus Magnusson and Hermann Pálsson nearly every instance of the formula 'now the story must be told how . . .' or 'now the story must go back to . . .' tends to become: 'Meanwhile Unn . . .' or 'Meanwhile, Thorvald's companions . . .', or the like. Such are very acceptable renderings of what many people would regard as a clumsy turn of phrase in Icelandic. Yet this formula, which has the same function as Chaucer's

> And in this blisse lete I now Arcite,
> And speke I wole of Palamon a lite

was meant to pilot the listener through the intricacies of the story; and though the modern reader does not need such emphatic pointers that a change of scene is imminent, to be unaware of the existence of these signposts, and of the medieval listener's need for them, is surely a loss. More effective, in this respect, are the passages in the translations of Gwyn Jones, in which many Icelandic narrative formulae have been preserved in modern idioms:

And so all was quiet.

The story goes on to tell that Halla Lytingsdottir spoke one day with Brodd-Helgi . . .

We must here introduce a man by the name of Thorvard.

The next thing to tell of is that Thorkel sent a man . . . (*Eirik the Red and other Icelandic Sagas*, pp. 7, 50, 66 and 67)

But as every reader knows, the saga authors do more than simply adhere to traditional themes and formulae. These by themselves do not make a saga, but are merely the outward indications of the settled principles on which the authors present their stories, characters and judgments. The saga *genre* includes biography, history and chronicles, and to the restrained, objective approach required for works of this kind the saga authors stick even when their stories are largely or wholly fictitious. Accordingly, they carefully avoid giving the impression that they invent, and they claim no special knowledge of their characters or insight into their minds. We see these characters act and hear them speak; occasionally they reveal their emotions in a change of colour, a facial expression or a gesture. But their motives and feelings are never explained, and their true nature remains hidden behind their image in the eyes of 'the district', whose collective opinion usually contains the only explicit judgments made in the sagas. 'People thought...', 'most people would have it...' and 'all were agreed ...'—with such reiterated phrases the saga author refuses to commit himself, leaving the whole burden of judgment and interpretation to his readers.

The effectiveness of such objectivity and reticence is perhaps most strikingly seen, not in the biography of a king or the chronicle of a feud (where restraint and impartiality might be desirable qualities), but in a love story where, by any standards except those adopted by saga authors and their audience, they would seem out of place. Such a love story is *Laxdœla Saga*.

This is ostensibly a family chronicle, concerned with men who moved from Norway to Iceland and settled in Salmonriverdale, and with their descendants. The procession of events in the lives of these families moves past at an even pace, from episode to episode, from father to son; yet there is little doubt that all this is but setting and background to an episode which occupies less than a quarter of the saga: the story of Gudrun's love for Kjartan, her marriage to Bolli, and the burning jealousy which leads her to plan the destruction of the man she loves.

There is little in the actual structure of *Laxdœla Saga* to throw this episode into relief. The narrative is not noticeably speeded up or slowed down at any point; the account of how Kjartan is slain is no more circumstantial than the story of Kjartan's grandfather's Hoskuld, buying a slave woman, or of Kjartan's father,

Olaf Peacock's going to Ireland to claim his royal descent. Like a good family chronicler, the saga author appears to give us the facts and the personalities without subordinating one to the other, and yet he creates a curious perspective, in which Gudrun is always in focus while the representatives of other generations of Laxdalers seem a little blurred, and even the supposedly more colourful and romantic figure of the young Olaf Peacock stands in the wings, a man of less importance and lesser stature.

What contributes to this effect is not the figure of Gudrun as much as the nature of her predicament, which is almost identical with that of her legendary prototype, Brynhild. Brynhild likewise loved a man who would not marry her and so she destroyed him, using as her instrument the husband whom she did not love. The character of Gudrun undoubtedly gains by these associations.

There is, however, one significant difference between character and prototype: all the hatred, rage and sorrow which Brynhild expresses so eloquently in the *Poetic Edda*, Gudrun endures in tight-lipped silence. When Bolli tells her the story of Kjartan's friendship with Ingibjorg, the sister of the Norwegian king, Gudrun bravely declares that this is good news:

> Then she let the talk drop all of a sudden and went away and was very red in the face; but other people doubted if she really thought these tidings as good as she gave out she thought they were. (Muriel Press, *The Laxdale Saga*, pp. 145–6)

She marries Bolli while Kjartan marries Hrefna, and from then on suffers in silence the humiliating torture of unrequited love:

> In the morning one of the women on going down the hall was talking how the ladies would be shown to their seats. And just as Gudrun had come right against the bedroom wherein Kjartan was wont to rest, and where even then he was dressing and slipping on a red kirtle of scarlet, he called out to the woman who had been speaking about the seating of the women, for no one else was quicker in giving the answer, 'Hrefna shall sit in the high seat and be most honoured in all things so long as I am alive.' But before this Gudrun had always had the high

seat at Herdholt and everywhere else. Gudrun heard this, and looked at Kjartan and flushed up, but said nothing. (Ibid, pp. 160–1)

Remarkably enough, such constant reserve on the part of Gudrun and her creator does not result in coldness or lack of feeling; on the contrary, the impression of turbulent passions hidden behind a placid Icelandic exterior is very strong. Possibly this impression owes a good deal to the associations with the Eddic Brynhild. This, however, if true, offers no ground for criticism of the saga, since in the end it is not the resemblance between the two women which strikes us most, but the contrast. We may know the depth of Gudrun's suffering only because we know Brynhild's, but in a passage like the one quoted above, her unspoken anguish makes her seem more vulnerable and human than Brynhild was ever meant to be.

In this restrained and suggestive treatment of a legendary motif against the naturalistic background of eleventh-century Iceland, the saga author reveals his considerable gifts. But it is his last stroke which is remembered even by readers who have long forgotten the rest of the story: Gudrun's famous admission to her son Bolli, 'To him I was worst whom I loved best.' The fact that Gudrun is made to express her feelings only when she has reached old age, and can look back on them with a certain equanimity, is a striking enough instance of the saga author's love of objectivity and emotional restraint. But an even more striking instance of it are the words themselves, in which at the very end of the story the whole riddle of her being and conduct is summed up in an oxymoron.

The restraint is all the more remarkable for the presence in _Laxdœla Saga_ of innumerable colourful and romantic touches. Melkorka is an Irish princess, abducted by pirates and sold into slavery; when Hoskuld buys her from Gilli the Rich, she is poorly dressed like a beggarwoman, but in costly raiment her beauty is at once apparent. Her son, Olaf Peacock, sets out on a quest armed with three objects which prove his royal descent: a gold ring, a knife and a belt. After Kjartan's death, Hrefna dies of a broken heart. Gudrun, like Guenevere, becomes a nun in her old age. Examples of this kind, which seem straight out of fairy-tale or romance, could be multiplied.

But it is with these effects as with the emotions in this saga: they are never permitted to blossom into extravagance. Melkorka never returns to Ireland to live happily ever after in the splendour to which she was born. The dashing young prince, Olaf Peacock, in his maturity, turns out to be a sober and responsible farmer, whose wife belongs to one of the best families and whose livestock is so numerous that it could stretch in an unbroken line from Goddistead to Herdholt. Hrefna is only *said* to have died of a broken heart, and Gudrun, for all her spiteful and destructive acts, is no Guenevere. Moderation triumphs.

Muriel Press's translation of *Laxdœla Saga* was first published in 1899. Though not as famous as G. W. Dasent's translation of *Njáls Saga*, it has stood the test of time a good deal better than the translations made in the same period by William Morris and Eiríkr Magnússon in their *Saga Library*, (London, 1891–1905). Yet, in so far as it is possible to class them together in a nineteenth-century school of translators of Icelandic family sagas, Muriel Press's work belongs to it unmistakably: like the others, she keeps close to the idioms and style of her original, with great unconcern for the unusualness and even awkwardness which sometimes results. This boldness, compared with which the efforts of more recent translators seem a little timid and unenterprising, is often very successful, for much of her translation gives us a vivid impression of the directness and vigour of the saga narrative:

> . . . and as he jumped to land Thorolf happens to be standing near, and forthwith hews at him, and the blow caught him on his neck against the shoulder and off flew his head.

> Thorkell now comes to the hut, he sees where a man is sitting by the water at the mouth of a brook, where he was line-fishing, and had a cloak over his head. (*The Laxdale Saga*, pp. 31 and 202.)

With renderings like these, Mrs. Press constantly reminds her readers of the remarkable feature at the heart of this saga: the contrast between the tragedy and passion of the story, and the robust and unsentimental way in which it is told.

However, to accuse the post-nineteenth-century translators of timidity is to do them less than justice. It is true that the work of some of them seems a little colourless after the flamboyance of William Morris's translations, the heroic simplicity of Dasent's *Burnt Njal*, or the liveliness and immediacy of Muriel Press's *Laxdale Saga*. But the translations of these three amount, in varying degrees, to personal visions of the saga age and of saga literature, which the translators of today no longer share. G. W. Dasent's rendering of the Icelanders' terse, colloquial speech and common-sense proverbs often brings the characters of *Njáls Saga* admirably to life, but it also removes them to a far past. With his consistent use of *thou*, *thee* and *ye* and the verbal forms that go with them, and his archaic words and idioms, he emphasizes throughout that these characters are people of a bygone age. And so they were, indeed, even when the saga author first conceived the story. The age to which they belonged was one on which the author could look back with admiration as an age of independence, integrity and honour, a saddening contrast to his own century of corruption and deceit. It was, above all, this feeling about the past, a compound of pride in its heroism and regret for its passing, which G. W. Dasent tried to express in his translation of the saga.

But the author of *Njáls Saga* was not inclined to idealize the age of which he wrote. To him and to his audience this may have represented a heroic past, but it was also a past which could be made a vehicle for a great deal of comment on the present. This, of course, is a narrow appreciation of the saga author's aims; yet there is a moral behind this story of snowballing violence, even if it is never made explicit, and it cannot be summed up in half a dozen sentences without underrating the author's breadth of vision or his artist's instincts. The saga clearly reflects the experiences of a man who has seen the effects of too much violence on his own age; it is a story about people who are committed to it, frequently against their inclinations:

'But I wish I knew,' said Gunnar, 'whether I am any the less manly than other men, for being so much more reluctant to kill than other men are.' (M. Magnusson and H. Pálsson, *Njál's Saga*, p. 135)

In a man like Gunnar, whose heroic status has been firmly, if conventionally, established in Chapter 19, in the formal portrait with which he was introduced, such reluctance to kill is obviously not a sign of unmanliness, but a virtue, an ideal even. This ideal is reflected again in the distaste with which Flosi Thordarson performs his moral duty, the burning of Njal and his household. Above all, the ideal is embodied in the figure of Hoskuld Hvitaness-Priest, who admits that he would rather be killed by the sons of Njal than have to kill them himself, and rather fall unatoned than to cause suffering to others, (Chapter 109).

One needs little knowledge of life in medieval Iceland to realize the enormity of this. But it is the tragedy of all concerned, burners and burnt alike, that Hoskuld does not fall unatoned, as he himself would have preferred: after his death, a carefully negotiated settlement fails because of misunderstanding and wounded pride, so that, in the end, his killing is paid for with the burning at Bergthorsknoll.

Yet it is as if Hoskuld's meekness and his forgivingness at the moment of his death have, after all, left their mark on people. At the Althing, Hall of Sida declares that he is prepared to forego compensation for his son Ljot's death, if thereby he can put an end to the violence (Chapter 145). And in the last chapter, Njal's son-in-law Kari walks into the house of Flosi, the leader of the burners, and Flosi embraces him; that is how the feud and the saga end.

Part of the tragedy lies in the failure of the law. Practised with devotion, but regarded with misgiving because of its obvious shortcomings, the law provides men with an insecure bulwark against violence. When Snorri the Priest is asked whether the men who killed Hoskuld will be outlawed from the district or from the whole country, Snorri replies that they shall not be outlawed at all, 'for such sentences have often been disobeyed, and thus given rise only to further killings and further enmities.'

(Ibid., p. 253.) Yet the law is the Republic's only hope. When Njal is told that many people would prefer to settle their claims with weapons, his reply is unequivocal:

> 'That must never happen. . . . It would be quite wrong to have no law in the land.' (Ibid., p. 209)

This may sound like a commonplace, but the events of *Njáls Saga* show that it was not taken for granted. To settle a claim with weapons was often a surer way of settling it than by means of the law, and there were certain wrongs and insults which could only be wiped out with blood:

> 'Where are you off to, Skarp-Hedin?' he asked.
> 'To look for your sheep,' replied Skarp-Hedin.
> 'You would not be armed if that were your intention,' said Njal. 'You must have some other purpose.'
> 'We are going to fish salmon, father, if we cannot find the sheep,' said Skarp-Hedin.
> 'If that were true, it would be best not to let your catch escape,' said Njal. (Ibid., p. 116)

Even Njal, with his knowledge of and regard for the law, recognizes the need for efficient killing, that no intended victim may escape to take vengeance later on. But elsewhere he says:

> 'It is no breach of settlement . . . for a man to have lawful dealings with another. With laws shall our land be built up but with lawlessness laid waste.' (Ibid., p. 159)

From the lips of the prescient Njal, this last remark is no mere gnomic phrase but a prophecy of what will surely come to pass; in the saga author's day it had already happened.

To the reader of today, such allusions to thirteenth-century conditions and experiences cannot be as clear and pointed as they must have been to a contemporary audience. Yet, ideally at least, a translation should attempt to convey something of the same sense of immediacy and relevance as its original did. In this respect, the translation by Magnus Magnusson and Hermann Pálsson has, to us, twentieth-century readers, a decided advantage over G. W. Dasent's *Story of Burnt Njal*. Dasent's version, with its many archaisms, dialect words and literal renderings, seems throughout preoccupied with a past that has no bearing on the present. The new version, however, erects no barriers of vocabulary and syntax between the present and the past. On the contrary, its convincing, twentieth-century idioms bring the lives of the people in the saga startlingly close to our own, so that we recognize at once Bergthora's shrewish wit, the grinning, loutish modernity of Skarp-Hedin at his worst, the fierce temper and domineering will of Hallgerd—the only woman in the saga capable of showing her feelings with something like abandon.

The propositions put forward in *Njáls Saga*, that violence breeds violence, disastrously, but that the true hero is the man who is reluctant to kill, who would rather swallow his pride to achieve peace than go on killing to save his honour, are as valid today as they ever were, and needed restating in the language of our time. It is only when we come to the moments in the saga that are so extraordinary as to be for ever remembered, that G. W. Dasent's simple, heroic phrasing continues to haunt the memory:

They ride down along Markfleet, and just then Gunnar's horse tripped and threw him off. He turned with his face up towards the Lithe and the homestead at Lithend, and said, 'Fair is the Lithe; so fair that it has never seemed to me so fair; the corn fields are white to harvest, and the home mead is mown; and now I will ride back home, and not fare abroad at all.' (*The Story of Burnt Njal*, p. 131)

II

Medieval Poetry and the Visual Arts

ELIZABETH SALTER

A STRIKING feature of critical writing about medieval English
poetry in the last decade has been its increasing use of medieval art
not simply to elucidate or to confirm its references, but also to
clarify its principles of composition and, even further, to interpret
its meaning.

Three large areas of Chaucer's poetry have been examined in
terms of art: character-creation, setting and structure. The form
of the *Canterbury Tales* was 'substantially defined' in 1957 by
reference to art-historians, who were describing the aesthetics of
Gothic art.[1] A precedent had been established: recent studies of
'Gothic unity and disunity' in Chaucer have used the characteristics of Gothic art, and in particular, of Gothic architecture, as
the basis for analysis of a highly professional and rigorous nature.[2]
The whole of Chaucer's work has been placed for us in a cultural
context which owes as much to the researches of Panofsky as to
the theology of St. Augustine: D. W. Robertson's *A Preface to
Chaucer*[3] sets medieval art and literature in closest connection.
So, Chaucer's exuberance and seeming illogicality of procedure
are explained as features of a special English variety of 'Gothic',
and related to fan-vaulting and manuscript painting of the fourteenth century. Convention and realism in the make-up of many
of Chaucer's characters are defined, significantly, as 'iconography'
and 'delineation from life', and illustration is again drawn from
sculpture and manuscript painting. The problematic settings of

---

[1] Charles Muscatine, *Chaucer and the French Tradition* (University of California
Press, 1957), pp. 167–9.

[2] See R. M. Jordan, *Chaucer and the Shape of Creation: the Aesthetic Possibilities
of Inorganic Structure* (Harvard University Press, 1967).

[3] (Princeton University Press, 1963.) See, in particular, Chapter III, 'Late
Medieval Style'.

the *Canterbury Tales* are said to be the result of a 'typically Gothic disregard for spatial unity' and specific analogues are suggested— gold leaf for the empty settings, inconographic pictorial schemes for those of a more detailed kind.[1]

These analogies and, in some cases, identifications with the visual arts are as stimulating as they are wide-ranging, but they raise many questions. It would be unwise to assume that they can do much more than act suggestively, or evocatively, upon the reader; they cannot be used to provide exact proofs. While they should never be regarded as precision instruments, they may, in fact, turn out to be double-edged weapons of some peril, both for the critic and for the poetry he examines. This is not to say that even when they are wrongly applied they are useless; they may reveal unexpected truths which, although complex and inconvenient, will press for admittance.

We may take, for instance, the relating of character-creation and verisimilitude of setting in Chaucer's poetry to certain characteristics of Gothic art. It is a good corrective to the persistent view of Chaucer's characters as psychologically convincing and life-like to be reminded that their sudden lapses from dramatic realism and their retreat into stereotype not only occur, but are familiar and meaningful in terms of the isolating tendencies of Gothic art.[2] And it would have spared us a good many essays on 'character-contradictions' if direct communication with the listener or the viewer had been recognized as a natural medieval alternative to indirect communication via overheard or overseen words and actions—an alternative used frequently, with little or no explanation. Nothing could be a better warning of the danger of expecting consistent dramatic illusion in Chaucer's poetry, and of the flight to disappointment or to ingenuity which must follow, than the page of a fourteenth-century manuscript, or the sculpted front of a Gothic cathedral, the canopy of a Gothic tomb, with their figures of the Holy Family, Saints or Kings, juxtaposed but isolated from each other, gazing out of the spatial setting they share to some remote realm of truth, beyond us. So in an early

[1] Ibid., pp. 257–9.
[2] *A Preface to Chaucer*, p. 269.

fourteenth-century Psalter illustration,[1] the Virgin and St. Christopher, each with their divine burden, stand side by side in the same arcaded setting, but have no contact with each other; the mounded water in which St. Christopher stands almost laps the Virgin's robe, but she is insensible of it. They confront us directly with their separate roles in God's narrative. So, sometimes, Chaucer's characters, Walter and Griselda, Palamoun and Arcite, Criseyde, Troilus and Dorigen do not converse as much as speak out beyond their narrative setting with a consistency which is local and isolable, not part of a 'nexus of dramatic or psychological interactions'.[2] Dorigen's unlikely rehearsal of just a few of the 'thousand stories' she could tell about wronged women,[3] Criseyde's protestations of fidelity, when all hope of fidelity has gone,[4] are presented not so much for their naturalness in a particular human dilemma as for their appropriateness in an ideal moral situation.

And yet, for all that, Gothic art of the fourteenth century should help us to question the idea that what we instinctively and persistently register as 'realism' in Chaucer can be adequately described as skill in conversational English, and verisimilitude in detail of setting.[5] More than a 'sense of immediacy' is involved. For it is not simply an increasing degree of verisimilitude which we notice in some areas of fourteenth-century painting and sculpture. This in itself is impressive enough to make us uneasy about agreeing that 'realism was alien to the artistic expression of the period generally'.[6] Realism and formalism coexist, in art as in literature; a fourteenth century pattern-book, such as the *Pepysian Sketch Book*,[7] records among mythical, zodiacal and symbolic creatures, a whole world of English game and domestic animals, more closely observed, and naturally set than any in Chaucer's major or minor poems. Chanticleer, striking though he is when

[1] Corpus Christi College, Cambridge, MS. 53, the *Peterborough Psalter*, f. 16a.
[2] *A Preface to Chaucer*, p. 272.
[3] *Franklin's Tale*, ll. 1355–1455.
[4] *Troilus and Criseyde*, v. 1590–1631.
[5] *A Preface to Chaucer*, pp. 278–80.
[6] Ibid., p. 277.
[7] Magdalene College, Cambridge, MS. 1916.

first introduced to us, is most accurately associated with courtly
painting of elaborate French style—an art of hard, brilliant substance and formal stance:

> His coomb was redder than the fyn coral,
> And batailled as it were a castel wal;
> His byle was blak, and as the jeet it shoon; . . .
> And lyk the burned gold was his colour.[1]

The miniatures in an early fifteenth-century French manuscript,
containing a translation of Bartholomew the Englishman's *De
Proprietatibus Rerum*,[2] provide perfect equivalents; the cockerel
on folio 177 is closer to Chaucer's description of Chanticleer than
the cockerel of the *Pepysian Sketch Book*, which is a recognizable
farmyard bird. Here Chaucer's detail is meant to dazzle rather
than to convince by its familiarity. Only when he begins to
involve his bird-characters in action does he change to a mode of
naturalism: the edgy, amorous relationship of Chanticleer and
Pertelote is portrayed in rounded, human terms.

And here fourteenth-century art is still relevant: side by side
with patterns of isolation and juxtaposition, it shows us more
complex patterns of relationship—persons and objects in dramatic
inter-connection. A scene from a *Bohun Psalter*[3] of the later fourteenth century pictures Christ's journey to Calvary as an embry-
onic but moving drama of weariness and derision; an earlier
fourteenth-century *Peterborough Psalter* displays the whole Passion
sequence as a series of stylized events, held still in a luminous
spiritual atmosphere.[4] *The Lytlington Missal*,[5] made for an abbot
of Westminster between 1383-4, contains a crucifixion scene
packed with incident and movement of actors; the Job paintings
in St. Stephen's Chapel, of the same date, must, from what we
can still see, have been impressively dramatic in conception. So,
Chaucer's Griselda is not entirely Petrarch's emblem of patient

---

[1] *Nun's Priest's Tale*, ll. 2859-61, 2864.
[2] Fitzwilliam Museum, Cambridge, MS. 251.
[3] National Library of Scotland, MS. Adv. 18.6.5, f. 25b.
[4] Corpus Christi College, Cambridge, MS. 53, ff. 12a-15b.
[5] Westminster Abbey Library.

fortitude; occasional comments show her reacting sharply and directly to the cruelty of Walter's testing.[1] Criseyde and Pandarus engage in convincing manœuvres of inquiry and dissimulation.[2] Arcite and Palamoun are given formal, complementary speeches, but they also seize and capitalize on each other's words.[3]

There is, in fact, room in later fourteenth-century art and literature to accommodate the widest variety of expressive modes: the Italianate-English, dramatic styles of the *Bohun* manuscripts, of the *Lytlington Missal* and the paintings in St. Stephen's Chapel correspond to the even more highly developed dramatic styles to be found in Chaucer's *Troilus* and in parts of the *Canterbury Tales*. Having said this, we must admit that recession to other less dramatic methods is frequent in both painting and poetry; there is less dramatic interconnection between Criseyde and Troilus than between Criseyde and Pandarus. Chaucer's treatment of his hero is more formal by far. Consistency of procedure would not have recommended itself to the medieval artist or poet as much as variety. A fair reading of the *Clerk's Tale* or of *Troilus and Criseyde* depends upon our willingness to admit that the value of his symbolic material is frequently—though temporarily—obscured for Chaucer by his sense of dramatic immediacy,[4] and that the poems, like many fourteenth-century manuscripts, screen-paintings or tomb-canopies, are chequer-boards of styles and approaches. The art of his time cannot be used to support any particular theory about Chaucer as 'realist' or 'symbolic moralist', although it can suggest to us the complexity, and even the un-certainty, of the relationship between the two. While it will certainly not rule out the possibility that Chaucer's poetry is 'concerned primarily with ideas',[5] it will also indicate the possi-bility that some of his finest, and most original work might be in the field of 'dramatic or psychological interactions'.

On the vexed question of the backgrounds and settings of poetry, art is again an unpredictable ally. Attempts have been

[1] *Clerk's Tale*, ll. 852 ff.
[2] See the whole episode in Book II, ll. 85–595.
[3] *Knight's Tale*, ll. 1123 ff.
[4] See *A Preface to Chaucer*, p. 280.
[5] Ibid., p. 279.

made to explain the contrast between background emptiness or vagueness and foreground detail in both Chaucer and Langland by means of book-illumination and altar-painting—the 'floating' of religious subjects against gold, as in the *Avignon Piéta*, the *Wilton Diptych*, or in innumerable miniatures of the period.[1] But the comparisons will not stand scrutiny, and we are left feeling that gold leaf is a fashionable remedy for critical doubt about spatial concepts in the work of medieval poets. In the first place a background of gold leaf, or indeed, of gold paint, hardly ever gives an impression of emptiness; it is a very assertive feature of manuscript painting, whether used, with tooled decoration, as a back-drop of substantial splendour, recommending the pictured events of the foreground to the viewer, or in the case of religious subjects, as a symbolic comment upon their divine meaning and context:

> the glittering surface, which changes in brightness
> with the smallest movement on the spectator's part . . .
> effectively destroys all visual association with this
> world; it creates a celestial envelope of light, in
> which bodies have no corporeality . . .[2]

Neither function is relevant to the *Canterbury Tales*. If we are anxious to find a more exact parallel between painted backgrounds and the setting of Chaucer's poetry, we can point to the *Book of the Duchess* with its dream-description of a may-morning:

> And eke the welken was so fair,—
> Blew, bryght, clere was the ayr, . . .
> Ne in al the welken was no clowde . . .[3]

This is a precise verbal equivalent of another convention of

[1] Ibid., p. 258: 'the pilgrims might just as well be seen moving against a background of gold leaf'.

[2] R. Hinks, *Carolingian Art* (London, 1935) pp. 38–9.

[3] ll 339–40, 343: the whole passage is highly reminiscent of pictoral conventions—the 'glade gilde stremes' (l. 338) of the sun must surely refer to its gold-rayed appearance in manuscript painting.

medieval art—the intense, plain, blue background which is often an alternative to plain gold. The exquisite, formal landscapes illustrating Jean Corbechon's *Proprietez des Choses*[1] are frequently backed by 'blew, bryght, clere' and cloudless skies. In both cases, art and poetry, we are dealing with a visual and thematic convention, rather than with a version of naturalism. The purely decorative value of blue as a foil for landscape details in green, white and red is fully realized; there are also signs that it is used, like gold, to represent the changeless spiritual ether which backs and surrounds all created things. So, again, it cannot be said to give an effect of 'emptiness', if that is what we are seeking: it vibrates with deep colour and meaning. The clearest examples of this significant use of blue backing come from eleventh- and twelfth-century religious painting, from books such as the *Sacramentary of Limoges*[2] and the *Bury Bible*.[3] But in its extensive use by later medieval painters, in more naturalistic contexts, it is still possible to see symbolic and decorative purpose. Both are present, unmistakably, in the backing to Giotto's frescoes in the *Scrovegni Chapel, Padua*. Both can, perhaps, be discovered in the backing to the Calendar pictures of the *Très Riches Heures*, made for Jean, Duc de Berri, in the early fifteenth century: the deep blue of heaven, through which the chariot of the sun drives, and the constellations shine, passes imperceptibly to become the unchanging back-drop of man's seasonal pageant.[4] And in Chaucer's poem, a blue, bright, cloudless setting may symbolize something of the theme: consolation is offered not by disguising the fact of the death of the Duchess, but by presenting human fidelity in love in an ideal and changeless form.[5]

The background to the *Canterbury Tales* is at once a more and less complicated matter. Each of the *Tales* has, of course, its own setting and orientation; we are led to look at the world of each

[1] See p. 19 above.
[2] Bibliothèque Nationale, MS. Lat. 9438, made about 1100.
[3] Corpus Christi College, Cambridge, MS. 2, made between 1121 and 1148.
[4] Only in the picture for the month of February is there any serious attempt to render the wintry subtleties of the northern-European sky.
[5] See J. Lawlor, 'The Pattern of Consolation in *The Book of the Duchess*', Speculum, xxxi (1956).

one as through the open windows of many later medieval pictures —from the frame, the window-sill, we see a various landscape. But for the Canterbury Pilgrimage itself, with its stress—uneven, admittedly—upon points along a route rather than upon landscape, we should expect to find visual equivalents in medieval maps, rather than in paintings. We are dealing with something nearer to geography than landscape-description, although medieval maps sometimes seem to be a curious combination of the two, with cartographic and pictorial elements. The map of Great Britain, made about 1360, and known as the *Gough Map*[1] was a fourteenth-century traveller's guide, and could have been familiar to Chaucer. It provides fairly accurate information on the road-network of medieval England, based, it is thought, on well-tried itineraries between main cities; it also includes stylised 'vignettes' for towns and important castles, with spires, towers, crenellated walls and a few houses. Chaucer's references to particular places on the way to Canterbury are brief, but deliberate; the background is only empty in the same way as the background to a mapped-itinerary might be called 'empty'. It is to common knowledge of a map that he appeals.

Finally, we may turn from space to structure, and consider how the application of the structural principles of Gothic art to the *Canterbury Tales* can help to demonstrate the nature and the unity of the whole work. Comparisons with Gothic form in other branches of the arts are always instructive, but not always amenable to particular critical theories. Certainly the break-up of a total design into separate, juxtaposed units of composition, and the arrangement of such a structure as a 'sequential procession',[2] can be recognized as a familiar procedure and pattern in Gothic art and architecture. We meet it in the frontal designs of Gothic cathedrals, in the 'window-pages' of manuscripts of the thirteenth and fourteenth century, which dispose a continuous narrative into separate pictures, each framed—and therefore isolable—but set within a larger enclosing frame. An intricate

---

[1] Facsimile printed by the Oxford University Press, with Introduction by E. J. S. Parsons (1958).
[2] *Chaucer and the French Tradition*, p. 168.

piece of carving such as the *Neville Screen*[1] in Durham Cathedral, is based upon the same principles; with its series of elaborately-worked niches, surmounted by delicate spires and pinnacles, it is an essay in repetitious, co-ordinate design. It spans the nave, however, as an entirely convincing and confident whole work of art. But comparison of any of these with the *Canterbury Tales* produces as many problems as solutions. It is easy to see that the 'collection of stories', envisaged as a medieval art-form, must, basically, be a Gothic co-ordinate construction: Boccaccio's *Decameron*, the moral collections such as the *Book of the Knight of la Tour Landry*, and Chaucer's own *Legend of Good Women* use, in a very simple way, sequential techniques. The works build cumulatively, through their separate and equal parts, to full size. Essentially, then, it is possible to see a familiar pattern in Chaucer's collection of *Canterbury Tales,* each representing a well-received genre of medieval literature, and each part of a sequentially-ordered whole: the larger structure of the pilgrimage. If there were no more to the *Canterbury Tales* than a variety of tales told at various points along a journey, and illustrative of the entire range of medieval taste and experience, we could legitimately compare them with other examples of Gothic art, to discover a unity which accommodates discrete parts: 'the basic structural procedure . . . is the inorganic one of additive collocation'.[2]

But in fact the *Canterbury Tales* is much more difficult to describe and account for than this would suggest. Much hinges upon the need of the present-day critic to find 'unity' in the whole work. But it is worth remembering that the concept of unity is far more flexible for the medieval period than for our own: even its desirability is not always apparent. In some ways, the skeleton structure of the *Canterbury Tales* is very similar to that of the manuscript collection of diverse materials—the 'miscellany', which had no other reason for existing than its diversity of content. While some collections work to a particular theme, others are built up simply on the principle of variousness. The fourteenth-century

---

[1] Given to the Cathedral in 1380, by Lord John Neville.
[2] *Chaucer and the Shape of Creation*, p. 238.

Vernon manuscript is an example of the first type, all of its contents gathered under one general heading, 'Salus anime, and in englyhs tonge Sowlehele'. Of the second type, there are innumerable examples from the fourteenth and fifteenth centuries: British Museum MS. Additional 16165, written by the fifteenth century 'publisher', John Shirley, has everything from treatises on hunting and on the Passion to Chaucer's translation of Boethius and love-complaints. It would be perverse to discuss the 'unity' of the *Vernon* manuscript except in the most general thematic terms and even more perverse to discuss that of the miscellany proper, although all could be said to illustrate, in a very free way, the medieval tolerance of a compendious structure (which may be no more than the material entity of the manuscript itself) of extremely various parts. There is less pressure upon the medieval writer than upon later writers to demonstrate over-all unity by any sort of cohesive methods; there is also no very sharp distinction between the compiler of materials written by others, and the creative artist.

The relevance of this to the *Canterbury Tales* is cautionary; we must beware of assuming it necessary to prove the unity of the whole composition by sophisticated aesthetic theory, since it is possible that Chaucer felt himself to be more in the position of the compiler of a miscellany than, for instance, in that of the architect of a Gothic cathedral. He may, in any case, have been more casually concerned with what, to later ages, has become a compelling problem—unification. His *Legend of Good Women* is a work which stands low in modern critical estimation for the mechanical way in which it brings together a collection of stories about unfortunate women, and for the rather listless execution of the scheme. It is doubtful whether medieval readers had any of our reservations about the crudity of the formal structure, any more than they had reservations about the structure of a collection of Saints' Legends, each accompanied by its commemorative picture of Saint and symbol.

But, of course, the *Canterbury Tales* is a very different proposition from the *Legend of Good Women*. Chaucer deliberately encourages us to think of it as more than just a miscellany of stories, or as a panoramic survey of the variety of medieval life. The *General Prologue*, with its announcement of dramatic verisimilitude in the telling of the *Tales*,[1] the reinforcement of this in the *Miller's Prologue*,[2] and the provision of the Links to the *Tales* raise different expectations, and set up different standards of judgment. While no one could deny that these innovations of Chaucer's inspired his finest dramatic writing, they also involved him in serious problems of organization. Left as a 'miscellany' with a purely formal introduction, the *Canterbury Tales* would, indeed, have invited straightforward comparisons with other fourteenth-century art forms, or with the manuscript compilation, for its principles of construction and its concepts of unity. As it comes down to us, it is a far more complex work, and, if it invites comparison with medieval art, takes us to fields in which the proof of unity is a far more hazardous activity.

For it is not only the marked fluctuation of literary quality in the *Canterbury Tales*—the *Second Nun's Tale* against the *Clerk's Tale*, the *Parson's Tale* against the *Pardoner's*—which should make us uneasy about comparisons with examples of Gothic art in which technical excellence is sustained throughout all parts of the design: the west-front of Wells Cathedral, the *Neville Screen*, the *Psalter* of Robert de Lisle.[3] We might, however, expect the 'unity' of a painted manuscript page or of a cathedral front to be questioned if the standard of workmanship varied as much as that of the *Tales*. We can go further than this, and ask whether there is not a more serious kind of fluctuation in the *Canterbury Tales*—a fluctuation of purpose, described conveniently, though crudely, as an uncertain movement between narrative and dramatic principles of organization. If this is true, it does not rule out the propriety of comparison with some forms of Gothic art, but not, on the whole, with those which manifest unity of composition most strikingly.

The characteristics of Gothic art after 1400 have been described

---

[1] ll. 725–36.

[2] ll. 3170–5.

[3] British Museum MS. Arundel 83, a composite *Psalter*, finely illuminated between *c.* 1300 and 1339.

Miniature from the early fifteenth century *Hours of Marguerite of Orleans.*

Bibliothèque Nationale, MS.Lat. 1156B, f.25ᵃ, reproduced in *Chefs-d'œuvre de l'Enluminure française*, présentés par J. Porcher (Les Editions Nomis, Paris), pl.ix.

as 'unbalance . . . conflict . . . disintegration of elements . . . lack of coherence'.[1] But even before 1400 it had shown signs of such tendencies. One department alone of English fourteenth-century art—that of manuscript illumination—often poses us the problem of deciding whether the written and decorated page is still a total artistic unit, or has already begun to disintegrate. 'Conflict and unbalance' are as often properly descriptive of the relationship between parts of the whole decorative scheme as 'diversity within unity'. We are not yet at the point when the border designs threaten to dominate the page entirely, taking precedence over the main picture and invading even the area originally reserved for the script: that will come, in the next century. But a number of elements are clearly in conflict in some manuscript painting of the fourteenth century—the Luttrell Psalter,[2] the Grey-FitzPayn Hours[3] show, beside pages where text, main picture and border design are relevantly balanced and linked, pages where border designs admit interest, in artist and patrons, difficult to interpret as anything but secular, dramatic, even comic by nature, and therefore intrusive.

Much effort has been expended upon proving that such secular 'irrelevances' are, in medieval terms, symbolically relevant. But we tread dangerous ground here if we are not prepared to consider the whole field of manuscript painting. It is dangerous to resort to ingenious symbolic explanations, in order to make disparate kinds of subject matter on a page of manuscript illumination exact echoes of each other.[4] For the manuscripts in which an 'implicit relationship' between main initial picture and border decoration can be shown to exist, an equal number, of the same date, deny such a relationship. The lavishly decorated Metz Pontifical,[5] of the earlier fourteenth century, uses the widest variety of marginal subjects, some overtly religious, some problematic, and some certainly secular. The relationship of border to initial picture is not particularly meaningful—initials taking standard types of subject

---

[1] Chaucer and the French Tradition, p. 245.
[2] British Museum MS. Additional 42130, made before 1340.
[3] Fitzwilliam Museum, Cambridge, MS. 242, made about 1308.
[4] A Preface to Chaucer, pp. 251–2.
[5] Fitzwilliam Museum, Cambridge, MS. 298.

which offer no scope for comparison, implicit or explicit, with the often wildly imaginative marginal subjects.[1]

But it is not only in subject-relationship that the illustrative schemes of fourteenth-century book painting exhibit conflicting elements; space-concepts are also a problem. As such schemes become more ambitious in scope, the problem of unifying the 'space-illusion' for the whole page of text, central-picture and margin becomes more acute. The 'inner conflict between the conception of the book-page as a primarily planimetric organism and its treatment as an opening into a recession of depth'[2] was only ever partially resolved by French and English artists of the fourteenth century. It is not uncommon to find sharp differences of viewpoint, scale and perspective, with margin and main subject unrelated, in spatial terms, to each other, and to the flat surface of the page of text.[3] The room for manœuvre was wide; in one powerful fifteenth-century attempt at a solution, the framing border is deliberately given an intensity of focus denied to the central scene—even when that scene is of the Crucifixion: 'we get the illusion that the marginal zone is alive, and the scene in the centre only a picture'.[4]

An increasingly dispersive relationship between the components of the manuscript page might indeed be expected from what we know of the changing conditions under which book painting was carried out during the fourteenth century. By the middle years, the secular and professional *atelier* had come to stay and there are many clear cases of division of labour—the text written in a monastic centre, but its illustration and decoration carried out by secular artists, to the demands of a lay patron.[5] Such circumstances do not strongly favour unity of design and theme—not even unity of opposed but meaningful parts. They

[1] See the Roxbrughe Club edition of the *Pontifical*, ed. F. S. Dewick (London, 1902), for detailed descriptions of the decorative schemes.

[2] O. Pächt, *The Master of Mary of Burgundy* (London, 1948), p. 25.

[3] See O. Pächt, 'A Giottesque Episode in English Medieval Art', *J.W.C.I.*, VI (1943), p. 52.

[4] *The Master of Mary of Burgundy*, p. 28.

[5] See D. D. Egbert, 'The Grey FitzPayn Hours', *Art Bulletin*, xviii, no. 4 (1936), p. 531 ff.

can, at worst, encourage a self-willed, somewhat indulgent diversity. The *Pepysian Sketch Book*[1] gives evidence of the profusion of decorative material which the fourteenth-century book-painter was expected to be able to provide for his patron's tastes— dogs hunting, cats washing, pheasants and mallards, rabbits, dragons, mermaids, saints, zodiacal beasts and a Pelican in its Piety. And a manuscript such as the *Grey-FitzPayn Hours*, which we know to have been decorated by lay artists, confirms that such tastes were successfully met.

If we take a wider view of Gothic art, looking not only at architecture of the high Gothic period, but at painting over the span of the Gothic centuries, it is impossible to deny that the basic structural principle of 'additive collocation' with its inevitable 'detachability of parts',[2] could only too easily result in disparity and unbalance of parts. The fifteenth century did, in fact, see 'the breakdown of the aesthetic equilibrium of Gothic book decoration'[3] but the warning signs of the breakdown were already apparent in Chaucer's day and earlier.

The importance of this to the *Canterbury Tales* is considerable. Chaucer's problem in that work of multiple parts is, like that of the book-painters, one of accommodation—of new materials, forms and impulses with older. 'Additive collocation' describes the various *Canterbury Tales*—juxtaposed, opposed, illustrative in content and genre of the variety of the medieval world. It cannot properly describe their frame, and their relationship with it—a relationship of pilgrim and tale which is, by turns, brilliantly maintained as dramatic illusion, halting and uncertain, and even non-existent. The *General Prologue* and, even more, the Links to the *Tales* draw upon sources of material and energy quite untapped by other medieval poets, and, perhaps, by any poet before Shakespeare. And as fourteenth-century illuminators often found licence, in their border-work, to experiment fruitfully with new dramatic themes and forms,[4] so Chaucer innovated,

[1] Magdalene College, Cambridge, MS. 1916: see p. 18 above.
[2] *Chaucer and the Shape of Creation*, p. 239.
[3] *The Master of Mary of Burgundy*, p. 19.
[4] See examples of this in the border designs of Jean Pucelle; K. Morand, *Jean Pucelle* (Oxford, 1962), p. 16.

unchecked, in his 'borders' to the *Tales*. Our anxiety to praise Chaucer should not prevent us from recognizing the unique nature of what he—imperfectly—attempted: the creation of 'free-standing characters' who could as actors function before an audience. The creation of the Wife of Bath involved Chaucer in something akin to the dramatists 'imaginative feat of detach-ment';[1] this urge to give independent life to characters, although it was frequently withdrawn, or hesitatingly offered, is the final distinguishing mark of Chaucer's art. It distinguishes the *Canterbury Tales* from the *Legend of Good Women* and from the *Confessio Amantis*, as it distinguishes *Troilus and Criseyde* from *Il Filostrato*.

But we cannot pretend that it makes for balance and unity. Its vehemence is liable to erupt through older surfaces, to disturb older patterns with sudden improvisation, as the Canon and his Yeoman gallop to join the pilgrimage, the Cook and Maunciple brawl, and the Wife of Bath so takes control of her *Prologue* that it ceases to be a medieval 'confession' and persuades us to speculate about hidden motive, and partially-revealed nature: 'the unfocused aspects of character work within the minds of those who encounter them, like yeast in bread'.[2] The powerful effort to evoke the pilgrims and their world in the Links, and sometimes in individual *Prologues* is more often abandoned than sustained in the *Tales*: we may compare the depth of focus in the portrait of the monk, in the 'merry words of the Host to the monk' with the flat mode of the *Tale*. It is a testimony to the vigour of these creations that critics have always been active to disguise difficulties by elaborate theories of dramatic irony, and, more recently, by theories of 'Gothic juxtaposition'. But these are false resolutions of the central problem, which is one of proportion and equilibrium. Like many illuminated pages of later medieval books, the *Canterbury Tales* does not properly adjust border material to main subjects. The frame, like the wide, packed, and errant borders of many manu-scripts, contains or fails to contain, an explosive life of its own secular, and dramatic; such a life advances upon the more static

---

[1] M. C. Bradbrook, *The Rise of the Common Player* (London, 1962), p. 128.
[2] M. C. Bradbrook, *English Dramatic Form* (London, 1965), p. 13.

and conventional material of many of the *Tales*, encroaching, without ever bidding for complete take-over.

That Chaucer might allow this to happen, we might predict from the statements of dramatic intent in the *General Prologue* and in the *Prologue* to the *Miller's Tale*. These should not be taken as humorous disclaimers of art[1] but, on the contrary, as serious passages, laying claim to art of a particular nature—that art of the dramatist which 'involves a kind of abdication'.[2] That Chaucer would not wish, or be able, to take a fully dramatic view of all of his material, we might also predict, from what we know of his immediate environment, and of the limitations imposed upon him by his age and training. But as in many later medieval book paintings, the uneasy tensions in the *Canterbury Tales* between different sorts of material and different approaches, the conflicts between narrative statement and dramatic exploration are defining elements in the make-up of the whole work.

The freedom for dramatic experiment allowed to the illuminators in the marginal area of their pages can often be proved to bear fruit, finally, in the increased liveliness of central page compositions.[3] It is doubtful whether, without the possibility of experiment in the frame-space, Chaucer's superbly complex presentation of the Wife of Bath, in her own *Prologue*, would have been achieved. This *Prologue* very decidedly represents the invasion of a narrative area by dramatic forms; the subsequent *Tale* is a mere appendage to what can only be described as a mature character-study. Similarly, in the whole relationship of border to main subject, frame to *Tale*, Chaucer and the illuminators often give us the impression 'that the marginal zone is alive, and the scene in the centre only a picture'. The many qualitative contrasts of pilgrim portraits, Links and *Tales* are not always to be dismissed as 'Gothic paradox', or 'juxtaposition of contrasting parts': they tell us of a problem of adjustment, rather than of a mastery of the problem. In a miniature from the early fifteenth-century *Hours*

[1] See *Chaucer and the Shape of Creation*, p. 122.
[2] *The Rise of the Common Player*, p. 128.
[3] See above, p. 29.

of Marguerite of Orleans,[1] the opening words of the prayer, 'Obsecro te domina', are accompanied by a picture of the countess, kneeling in front of the Virgin and Child. The scene is gorgeously but flatly presented, the group backed by ornate, glittering fabrics, their attitudes still and formal. But almost encircling prayer and picture, in a deep and profuse border, is a pilgrimage: knights, ladies on horseback, palmers on foot travel a winding road, through little woods, past flowers and butterflies, to a chapel, and beyond that, to the spires of a distant town. The pilgrimage is, indeed, 'alive . . . the scene in the centre only a picture': the world of the border is fully-dimensioned, and vigorously presses against the enclosed area of prayer and picture, as if it can hardly be contained. Drama restlessly stalks narrative over the manuscript page.

[1] See Plate facing p. 26.

III

Rant and Cant in 'Troilus and Cressida'

PATRICIA THOMSON

QUESTIONING the Duke of Edinburgh's faith in 'Word-Power',[1] an anonymous writer has recently asked: 'is not our own society, at least, one in which fluency remains a somewhat suspect achievement, in love as much as in politics?'[2] Society under Elizabeth I, with rhetoric a recognized study in grammar school and university, was very much less sceptical. The modern reader may therefore sometimes, unhistorically, suspect a Word-Power in which Shakespeare believed. Henry V, for instance, exemplifies in council and in war the true eloquence of a leader whose thoughts and actions always match his words and whose 'sweet and honey'd sentences' are justly appraised as virtuous adjuncts of the royal character (*Henry V*, I. i. 50): on a priori grounds, if none other, an Elizabethan would probably resist L. C. Knights's opinion that the speech before Harfleur is 'rhetorical in the bad sense'.[3] Passionate rhetoric at passionate moments, Shakespeare's forte, holds its own throughout the Renaissance. What its study did make educated men of his time aware of was passionate rhetoric in excess of its occasion and in trite forms. In other words, rant and cant, of all kinds, 'in love as much as in politics', were highly suspect:

> I see not one of these petty-ballad-makers, or prentise-dogrell rymers, that doth not bumbast his labors with high swelling and heaven-disimbowelling wordes . . . It is natural, simple, and vnaffected speach that I love. (Montaigne, *The Essayes*, trans. Florio, 1603, p. 83)

[1] See *Communication*, H.R.H. The Duke of Edinburgh's Presidential Address to The English Association 1968.

[2] *The Times Literary Supplement*, 18 July 1968, p. 753.

[3] *Shakespeare: the Histories*, London, 1962, p. 43.

The style-consciousness of the educated Elizabethan is well
exemplified in Hamlet. He is a connoisseur of drama, delighting,
though not uncritically, in an impromptu recitation. He is quick
to detect the courtly cant of 'this waterfly' Osric, and, in a note-
worthy passage, the would-be tragic rant of his rival Laertes:

> O! treble woe
> Fall ten times treble on that cursed head
> Whose wicked deed thy most ingenious sense
> Depriv'd thee of. Hold off the earth awhile,
> Till I have caught her once more in mine arms.
> Now pile your dust upon the quick and dead,
> Till of this flat a mountain you have made,
> To o'ertop old Pelion or the skyish head
> Of blue Olympus.   (*Hamlet*, V. i. 253-61)

These histrionics at the grave-side of Ophelia create a sense of
distrust, alienating sympathy where sympathy is in some part due.
Though Laertes has some affection for his sister and some cause to
hate her persecutor, neither is great enough to make his demand
to be buried alive convincing. He is not fully sincere. He is
emotional rather than passionate, so that his extravagant language,
coupled with his theatrical leap into the grave, antagonizes the
audience as much as it does Hamlet:

> What is he whose grief
> Bears such an emphasis? whose phrase of sorrow
> Conjures the wandering stars, and makes them stand
> Like wonder-wounded hearers?
>
> Dost thou come here to whine?
> To outface me with leaping in her grave?
> Be buried quick with her, and so will I:
> And if thou prate of mountains, let them throw
> Millions of acres on us, till our ground,
> Singeing his pate against the burning zone,
> Make Ossa like a wart! Nay, an thou'lt mouth,
> I'll rant as well as thou.   (V. i. 261-4, 284-91)

Troilus and Cressida, near neighbour in time to *Hamlet*, was
written probably about 1601-2 and in print in 1609. It is at least

equally alert to rant and cant, a fact which will seem the more appropriate if, as has been suggested,[1] it was written for the educated, style-conscious audience of the Inns of Court. The publisher of the first quarto, who definitely aims at the intellectual élite, boosts it as the wittiest of Shakespeare's comedies, comparing it favourably with the best of Terence and Plautus. And if, in view of the catastrophes of Act V, it is difficult to follow him the whole way, the first four acts are, undeniably, 'passing full of the palme comicall'. The extremes of style, ranging from the grand verse and Latinate idiom of Agamemnon, Nestor and Ulysses to the colloquial and often bawdy prose of Cressida, Pandarus and Thersites, are easily noticed. But it requires a Hamlet or an Inns of Court man to tell us whether the former is as comic as the latter and whether the constant inflation and deflation should dispose us to react to the play as to *Oh, What a Lovely War*. Most difficult to gauge is the effect intended by some of the 'serious' verse, which is suspect as rant or cant not so much because it is ridiculous in itself as because it adorns a story unlike that of *Henry V*—a story of a futile war 'in a bad cause' (II. ii. 117). Again the rhetoric is sometimes like Laertes's in that it creates distrust and alienates sympathy; but we are not always sure whether, with his, it should be jeered unceremoniously out of court. Nevertheless, there are obviously laughable instances, as, for example, the inflated description of Helen, 'the mortal Venus, the heart-blood of beauty, love's indivisible soul' (III. i. 33–4), which is given by Paris's page immediately before she is seen on stage, for the first and last time, as a remarkably silly woman: 'Let thy song be love; this love will undo us all. O Cupid, Cupid, Cupid!' (110–11) This suggests that, however rich in jokes appropriate only to the educated, *Troilus and Cressida* also relates to popular and ordinary comedy. Its effects are, in fact, found elsewhere in Elizabethan drama, and Shakespeare himself also here both builds on his earlier and anticipates his later practice. With these popular practices it is perhaps best to begin.

If the attack on the 'high swelling' and 'affected' was led by the

---

[1] By Peter Alexander in '*Troilus and Cressida, 1609*', *Library*, ix (1929), 267–86.

educated, it was probably followed up by the uneducated: the witty asides of common men, Dick and Smith, puncture the theatrical pomposity, and hence the pretensions, of 'We John Cade, so termed of our supposed father' (2 Henry VI, IV. ii. 33). Besides, the most obvious form the attack takes, which is parody, was not, to judge by its prevalence in comedy, caviar to the general. The 'huff-snuff' of Huanebango in The Old Wives' Tale is laughable, even if its particular targets, Stanyhurst and Harvey, are not distinctly recognized. The cant of knight-errantry with which Puntarvolo woos his wife in Everyman Out of his Humour is a popular Elizabethan joke. It recurs in The Knight of the Burning Pestle (c. 1609), which also parodies the rant of The Spanish Tragedy (c. 1587), by then old-fashioned.

Rant and cant, throughout Shakespeare's career and whatever his audience, serve the purposes of his comedy and satire. The parodies of antiquated dramatic bombast in A Midsummer Night's Dream and Henry V substantiate criticism through laughter. Bottom in 'Ercles' vein', though innocently funny, also exposes his own vanity and folly. Pistol, with the same vices in more objectionable form, exposes his character as chief of the 'three swashers' who follow the warrior king to France through such fake 'Senecan' verbosity as

> 'Solus' egregious dog? O viper vile!
> The 'solus' in thy most mervailous face;
> The 'solus' in thy teeth, and in thy throat,
> And in thy hateful lungs, yea, in thy maw, perdy;
> And, which is worse, within thy nasty mouth!
> I do retort the 'solus' in thy bowels.
> (Henry V, II. i. 48–53)

The joke at the expense of absurd characters is sometimes amplified by mimicry. 'My daughter! O my ducats! O my daughter!' (The Merchant of Venice, II. viii. 15): Solanio ridicules Shylock's excesses by an imitation so accurate that, though its effect is similar, it is hardly to be classed as parody.

These ranters anticipate Ajax, most foolish of the many fools in Troilus and Cressida:

Agamemnon: Give with thy trumpet a loud note to Troy,
Thou dreadful Ajax, that the appalled air
May pierce the head of the great combatant
And hale him hither.
Ajax: Thou trumpet, there's my purse.
Now thy lungs, and split thy brazen pipe;
Blow, villain, till thy sphered bias cheek
Outswell the choller of puffed Aquilon.
Come, stretch thy chest, and let thy eyes spout blood.

(IV. v. 3–10)

Agamemnon's praise of this 'dreadful' Greek champion is obviously as ironic here as it has been earlier (II. iii. 147–9), and, to match it, his order is intentionally inflated. Ajax, vain and stupid enough to miss the mockery, answers in kind: in the only book-length study of the play's style, his rant is justly compared to Pistol's.[1] It is the more absurd in its context, for, as the deflator Ulysses remarks, 'No trumpet answers' (12). There is a long pause, filled with the frivolous arrival of Cressida, before Hector, delayed by her departure from Troy, arrives to keep his appointment with Ajax. A further anti-climax follows, for their duel rapidly dissolves into friendly back-slapping: 'the issue is embracement' (148). So passes, as part of a great comic scene, Ajax's brief and only moment of verbal glory. For usually he is inarticulate, capable of little more than vituperative exclamations (as in II. i), of crude threats provoking his friends to mocking asides (II. iii. 200 f.), and of the meaningless 'Hum!' and 'Ha!', so brilliantly mimicked by Thersites when he 'puts on the presence' of this 'languageless . . . monster', who 'raves in saying nothing' (III. iii. 247 f.).

The intelligent, by contrast with the fools, make rant, with mimicry or parody, weapons of mockery. Falstaff in 'King Cambyses' vein' is much less innocent than Bottom in Ercles', for he is also guying King Henry's vein (*1 Henry IV*, II. iv. 382). In impudence and *lèse-majesté* he anticipates those more dangerous rebels against authority and order, Achilles and Patroclus. Ulysses

---

[1] Karen Schmidt di Simoni, *Shakespeare's 'Troilus and Cressida'. Eine sprachlich-stilistische Untersuchung* (Heidelberg, 1960), p. 106.

alerts the Greek leaders to the dangers of faction by means of an uncomfortably vivid description of Achilles 'mocking our designs', applauding the 'ridiculous and awkward action' with which Patroclus 'pageants us':

> Sometime, great Agamemnon,
> Thy topless deputation he puts on,
> And, like a strutting player whose conceit
> Lies in his hamstring, and doth think it rich
> To hear the wooden dialogue and sound
> 'Twixt his stretched footing and the scaffoldage,
> Such to-be-pitied and o'er-wrested seeming
> He acts thy greatness in; and, when he speaks,
> 'Tis like a chime a-mending; with terms unsquared,
> Which, from the tongue of roaring Typhon dropped,
> Would seem hyperboles. At this fusty stuff,
> The large Achilles, on his pressed bed lolling,
> From his deep chest laughs out a loud applause,
> Cries 'Excellent! 'tis Agamemnon right!
> Now play me Nestor: hem, and stroke thy beard,
> As he being dressed to some oration.'
>
> (I. iii. 151–66)

Once roused, Achilles can also behave 'like a strutting player' himself. Reducing Hector's challenge to 'trash', he seems on the verge of pageanting its chivalric terms (II. i. 120–5). More distinctly, in his message to Ajax, he out-tongues 'roaring Typhon' in an attempt to discredit the persons and manners he despises:

> Tell him I humbly desire the valiant Ajax to invite the most valorous Hector to come unarmed to my tent, and to procure safe-conduct for his person of the magnanimous and most illustrious six-or-seven-times-honoured captain-general of the Grecian army, Agamemnon et cetera. (III. iii. 272–7)

Nevertheless, being less clever, witty and good-natured than Falstaff, Achilles succeeds chiefly in discrediting himself as a sarcastic and therefore unreliable commentator. His own crude mimicry of the high style, with Patroclus's 'fusty stuff', resembles its extreme opposite, the low railing of Thersites, in one respect:

most of the mud slung bespatters the slinger. His travesty of
Agamemnon as a futile hyperbolist is to be classed with Iago's
equally despicable one of the eloquent and just Othello, who has,
supposedly, vociferated in favour of the wrong officer,

> with a bombast circumstance
> Horribly stuff'd with epithets of war.
> (*Othello*, I. i. 13–14)

This is not to deny that Achilles and Iago do damage. Unfor-
tunately, everything, including the noble dignity of Agamemnon's and Othello's utterance, is grist to the mill of these cynics.

The grist in Agamemnon's case is that, especially in the council
scene, that is, when a state of emergency is under discussion, he
speaks *too* nobly:

> Why then, you princes,
> Do you with cheeks abashed behold our works,
> And call them shames, which are indeed nought else
> But the protractive trials of great Jove
> To find persistive constancy in men? (I. iii. 17–21)

The same is true of his senior councillor Nestor, who always
tends, in any case, to echo the voice of the last speaker:

> With due observance of thy godlike seat,
> Great Agamemnon, Nestor shall apply
> Thy latest words. In the reproof of chance
> Lies the true proof of men, etc. (I. iii. 31–3)

Robert Kimbrough's objection that Agamemnon's speech is
'aloof, learned' is acceptable, but in adding that it 'signifies very
little'[1] he goes too far for some readers. The speech, arguing
cogently that true virtue does not blench at misfortune, is by no
means all sound and fury. The speaker urges his philosophy, as
G. Wilson Knight points out, 'with warmth and feeling', and
this more moderate and sympathetic judge is surely right to stop
criticism short with the observation that Agamemnon betrays a

---

[1] *Shakespeare's 'Troilus and Cressida' and its Setting* (Harvard U. P., 1964), p.
138.

'somewhat impractical mind'.[1] Again, Nestor's speech, though in
the nature of an elaboration of Agamemnon's and learnedly
adorned with allusions to Boreas, Thetis, Perseus and Neptune, is
far from senseless, so that it is not really satisfactory to sum up the
scene at this stage in the words 'All is rant so far—but rant
majestically phrased'.[2] These speeches can perfectly well be read as
samples of Elizabethan Word-Power inspired by moral feeling,
amiss only in that they are ill-adjusted to the military situation
seven years after the beginning of the siege of Troy. Perhaps they
reflect something of the war's protraction, and, in view of the
whole action of the play, Agamemnon and Nestor are certainly
right to stress chance rather than man's initiative as the operating
power in human affairs. In view of the military situation, however, the scene is certainly subject to criticism, even to ridicule, as
too slow-moving. Even Ulysses cannot immediately quicken its
tempo. Indeed, he chooses, probably deliberately, to slacken its
pace yet further, with those sixteen turgid lines of compliments
which form the only sound basis for Achilles's jeer: after the
ceremonies of

> Agamemnon,
> Thou great commander, nerve and bone of Greece,
> Heart of our numbers, soul and only spirit,   (I. iii. 54–6)

and so on, we are inclined to anticipate the arch-enemy's 'et
cetera'. Ulysses then ventures upon his famous oration on order
in the commonwealth, and so gradually brings the Greek leaders
down to matters nearer home than 'great Jove'. Ulysses's 'degree'
speech, which is too well known to quote, has itself recently
evoked such differences of opinion that one wonders whether,
for example, Karen Schmidt di Simoni, admiring its virtuosity
and brilliance as a speech of state, and Brian Vickers, denigrating
it as 'portentously diffuse', have been reading the same text.[3] The

---

[1] *The Wheel of Fire*, rev. ed. (London, 1959), pp. 49, 50.
[2] Kimbrough, p. 138.
[3] Schmidt di Simoni, pp. 72, 146; Brian Vickers, *The Artistry of Shakespeare's Prose* (London, 1968), p. 253. Kimbrough (p. 138), remarking on 'the forward press of active thought', joins the admirers, while J. Oates Smith (*P. Q.* xlvi

disagreement, which matches the current one on the whole issue of Word-Power and fluency, can probably not be settled—or could only be settled with the assistance of an original member of that hypothetical Inns of Court audience. Recognizing such commonplaces in Ulysses's political idiom as bees, planets, diseases and storms, he might be more prone than the ill-educated to think the speech platitudinous, which is the first step towards classing it as political cant comparable with today's 'nerve centres' and 'grass roots'. On the other hand, why should he not relish a genuine rhetorical urgency in the manner in which the speaker adapts commonplace ideas so long-windedly expounded by one of his predecessors? Compare the Archbishop of Canterbury's argument for division of labour in the commonwealth—

> for so work the honey-bees,
> Creatures that by a rule in nature teach
> The act of order to a peopled kingdom.
> They have a king and officers of sorts;
> Where some, like magistrates, correct at home,
> Others, like merchants, venture trade abroad,
> Others, like soldiers, armed in their stings,
> Make boot upon the summer's velvet buds;
> Which pillage they with merry march bring home
> To the tent-royal of their emperor.
>   (*Henry V*, I. ii. 187–96)—

with Ulysses's pointed rhetorical question:

> When that the general is not like the hive
> To whom the foragers shall all repair,
> What honey is expected?   (I. iii. 81–3)

Furthermore the message is not unimportant, for Agamemnon needs to be reminded that he is not 'like the hive': this is a way of

---

(1967), 177) condemns the 'bombastic quality' of Ulysses's language in the council scene. E. M. W. Tillyard, who originally found the 'degree' speech weighty (*The Elizabethan World Picture* (London, 1943), pp. 7–8), later took up a cautious middle position (*Shakespeare's Problem Plays* (London, 1950), p. 55), to which L. C. Knights's 'Commentators have perhaps been too much impressed by this piece of rhetoric' has lent some support (*Some Shakespearian Themes* (London, 1959), p. 68).

warning him that his leadership, unlike Henry V's, is ineffective. Nor is it to the point to contrast Ulysses's 'degree' speech with the later speech in which he urges Achilles to take Time by the forelock (III. iii. 145–89). In each case he argues *ad hominem*. Ironically, he succeeds in neither: Agamemnon does not become a strong leader, and Achilles's 'drowsy blood' is aroused, in the end, not by speeches but by the slaughter of Patroclus and the Myrmidons (V. v. 32–3). Ironies, however, do not turn speeches into speechifying. The dying John of Gaunt's advice to Richard II is not the less eloquent in that it passes unheeded.

The difficulty in knowing whether to take the various moral, political and military speeches as genuine or as phony oratory is only a little less great on the Trojan side. Even Hector, next to Ulysses the most persuasive speaker in the play, is suspect on one occasion. His argument, deduced from the 'moral laws of nature and of nations', for the return of Helen is as pressing and as little inclined to rant or cant as Ulysses's 'Time' speech. Yet it must seem hollow in view of the 'roisting challenge' which he has already sent to the Greeks, and, more particularly, in view of his immediate *volte-face*:

> Hector's opinion
> Is this in way of truth. Yet, ne'ertheless,
> My sprightly brethren, I propend to you
> In resolution to keep Helen still;
> For 'tis a cause that hath no mean dependence
> Upon our joint and several dignities.
> (II. ii. 188–93)

Such undermining makes utterances, sound in themselves, seem like rant. The effect is comic and deflationary, because Hector produces an anti-climax, speaking and acting against the noble convictions he has nobly expressed. His words cannot be taken seriously in context. Solemn as they are, they have no resonance within the play. Hector never speaks again with quite the same moral fervour. For he has voluntarily joined his irrational younger brothers, condoning Troilus's youthful storming about the worthless Helen:

> She is a theme of honour and renown,
> A spur to valiant and magnanimous deeds,
> Whose present courage may beat down our foes,
> And fame in time to come canonize us.
>
> (II. ii. 199–202)

His case is, in its way, pathetic. For just how strongly, in his heart, this greatest of the Trojans resists flamboyance of speech, is shown by his regret when Achilles momentarily goads him into it:

> For I'll not kill thee there, nor there, nor there;
> But, by the forge that stithied Mars his helm,
> I'll kill thee everywhere, yea, o'er and o'er.
> You wisest Grecians, pardon me this brag:
> His insolence draws folly from my lips;
> But I'll endeavour deeds to match these words.
>
> (IV. v. 254–9)

Fortunately, the play gives Hector a second chance on a lower moral plane. For if he has repudiated those 'moral laws' in which as a good Aristotelian he believes, he is at least allowed to act in accordance with the chivalric standards on which his self-respect as a gentleman depends. This knight errant has, however, his tongue in his cheek when he phrases his 'roisting challenge' to the Greeks.

Hector's challenge, delivered by Aeneas, provides the play's most notable example of the distrust created even by the suspicion of rant. Agamemnon's suspicions resemble Olivia's when she is assailed by Viola's rehearsed speech on her 'Most radiant, exquisite, and unmatchable beauty' (*Twelfth Night*, I. v. 174–5):

> *Aeneas:* Which is that god in office, guiding men?
>   Which is the high and mighty Agamemnon?
> *Agamemnon:* This Trojan scorns us, or the men of Troy
>   Are ceremonious courtiers. (I. iii. 231–4)

Here, it seems, is 'the tongue of roaring Typhon': Aeneas, without quite being 'saucy', is play-acting in the Achilles-Patroclus vein to which Agamemnon has at last been alerted. Agamemnon has his usual difficulty in tuning in to the immediate occasion. But once he has done so, he good-naturedly weighs in in the required

D

idiom. This idiom, a popular laugh-raiser, is, simply, the rant and cant of knight-errantry. For, even when allowance is made for the influence of Shakespeare's medieval sources (Chaucer, Lydgate, Caxton), he can hardly have intended this otherwise than as comic rant and cant:

> *Aeneas:* If there be one among the fair'st of Greece,
>   That holds his honour higher than his ease,
>   That seeks his praise more than he fears his peril,
>   That knows his valour and knows not his fear,
>   That loves his mistress more than in confession
>   With truant vows to her own lips he loves,
>   And dare avow her beauty and her worth
>   In other arms than hers—to him this challenge!
>   etc.

> *Agamemnon:* This shall be told our lovers, Lord Aeneas.
>   If none of them have soul in such a kind,
>   We left them all at home. But we are soldiers;
>   And may that soldier a mere recreant prove,
>   That means not, hath not, or is not in love!
>   (I. iii. 265–72, 284–8)

Ulysses caps it with a wry 'Amen'.

The 'ceremonious courtiers' of *Troilus and Cressida* are sometimes suspected of using meaningless cant terms which, in serious contexts, are perfectly acceptable, if common, social coinage. One such term is the complimentary 'sweet'. Gertrude shows decorum and delicacy when she calls Ophelia 'sweet maid', as does Horatio when he calls Hamlet 'sweet prince' (*Hamlet*, V. i. 252; V. ii. 359). On the other hand, the affected Armado makes it silly by over-use throughout *Love's Labour's Lost*, especially in his mincing talk with the courtiers he is unsuccessfully aping (V. ii). Pandarus does exactly the same in his inane boudoir-style conversation with Helen: 'Sweet queen, sweet queen; that's a sweet queen, i' faith ... What says my sweet queen, my very very sweet queen?' (III. i. 71, 79–80). Again, when Thersites debases this term he makes Hector sound insincere and Menelaus sordid:

Hector: Good night, sweet Menelaus.
Thersites: Sweet draught: sweet, quoth 'a! sweet sink, sweet
    sewer.   (V. i. 73–5)

Pandarus and Thersites both, in their different ways, do damage to
words, along with the things words signify. These two not only
lack dignity in themselves but destroy dignity in others: this is
also part of their function in the main love story.

The love story of *Troilus and Cressida* relates more particularly
to Shakespeare's idiom in his romance comedies. In these his
problem is to retain sympathy for the woeful lovers and belief
in their sincerity, without inducing so deep an involvement that
laughter and happiness are altogether banished from the audi-
torium. Here the rant and cant of love serve constantly and
successfully to preserve the comic tone in serious—or what could
be serious—moments of passion:

> Hang there, my verse, in witness of my love:
> And thou, thrice-crowned queen of night, survey
> With thy chaste eye, from thy pale sphere above,
> Thy huntress' name, that my full life doth sway.
>   (*As You Like It*, III. ii. 1–4)

Orlando, like Shakespeare's other young men in love, unwittingly
strikes conventional attitudes. And, though his attitudinizing
creates no distrust so disturbing as Laertes's, it too is subject to
ridicule. The audience cannot but share in the amused mockery,
the slight disillusion, at 'that fancy-monger', who 'abuses our
young plants with carving "Rosalind" on their barks; hangs odes
upon hawthorns, and elegies on brambles; all, forsooth, deifying
the name of Rosalind' (III. ii. 358–61).

The hero of *Troilus and Cressida* is, at the outset, a similar comic
hyperbolist and deifier of his mistress. The 'dexteritie, and power
of witte' admired by the publisher of the first quarto are never
more apparent than in the opening scene, a comic come-down
after the 'Prologue armed', with the love-sick Troilus discovered
unarming:

> Why should I war without the walls of Troy
> That find such cruel battle here within? (I. i. 1–2)

'Cruel battle', an Ovidian-Petrarchan cliché, immediately marks out another Elizabethan 'fancy-monger'. It is only the first of a series of cant terms and stock hyperboles of love, all of which are rendered more absurd by the tetchy Pandarus's puncturing, down-to-earth comments in prose. Troilus's invocations to the gods are high-wrought poeticisms:

> O gods, how do you plague me! (I. i. 96)
>
> Tell me, Apollo, for thy Daphne's love. (I. i. 100)

Love as a sea voyage (I. i. 51–3), as madness (53), as disease (55), as a wound (64), is familiar from the pages of that old Elizabethan favourite *Tottel's Miscellany*', whence Troilus could also have filched the phrase 'doubtful hope' (106).[1] Pandarus's detailing of Cressida's 'eyes, her hair, her cheek, her gait, her voice' (56), of which Troilus complains, followed by his own attempt to find ideal terms of comparison (57–61), is reminiscent of an Elizabethan catalogue of beauties, such as Spenser's *Amoretti*, no. 6. Pandarus's prosaic comparisons—'An her hair were not somewhat darker than Helen's', etc.—are obviously not good enough for a hyperbolist such as Troilus, who objects to such things as Cressida's beauty or Priam's greatness being weighed in 'a scale/Of common ounces' (II. ii. 27–8). So one of Shakespeare's favourite jokes occurs here in the extravagant eulogy of Cressida's hand:

> O, that her hand,
> In whose comparison all whites are ink
> Writing their own reproach, to whose soft seizure
> The cygnet's down is harsh, and spirit of sense
> Hard as the palm of ploughman. (I. i. 57–61)

Orlando swears 'by the white hand of Rosalind' (*As You Like It*, III. ii. 390–1). But it is Berowne who best exposes, by forswearing:

> Taffeta phrases, silken terms precise,
> Three-pil'd hyperboles, spruce affectation,
> 　　(*Love's Labour's Lost*, V. ii. 407–8)

---

[1] *Tottel's Miscellany*, ed. H. E. Rollins (Harvard U.P., 1928–9), no. 6.

to which he adds, with significant jocularity:

> and I here protest,
> By this white glove,—*how white the hand, God knows,*—
> Henceforth my wooing mind shall be express'd
> In russet yeas and honest kersey noes.   (411–14)

Troilus has not, however, yet reached the russet and kersey stage, and, left alone by Pandarus, is freer to soliloquize in the old vein. His final extravaganza (I. i. 97–102) has been correctly defined as in the Elizabethan sonnet style.[1] To Karen Schmidt di Simoni's comments it need only be added that the merchandise image, with Cressida as 'pearl' and Troilus as 'merchant', is no exception. Its associations are not, as sometimes supposed, mercenary. They are as traditionally lover-like and romantic as those of Spenser's 'Ye tradefull Merchants' (*Amoretti*, no. 15). It is not Troilus, but Pandarus, who is to talk of 'a bargain made' (III. ii. 96).

Though Troilus in the council scene is recognizably the same hyperbolist, with Helen taking Cressida's place as his 'pearl' (II. ii. 81), his language as lover undergoes a change when he is at last brought together with Cressida. Pandarus's chatter introduces a dumb-struck Troilus. 'You have bereft me of all words, lady' (III. ii. 53) is a phrase borrowed from Bassanio, who so receives Portia's declaration of love (*The Merchant of Venice*, III. ii. 176). And in both cases Shakespeare's psychology is sound. It is not merely that the moment of victory is overwhelming, or that effusiveness would be tasteless, but, as Pandarus says, 'Words pay no debts, give her deeds' (III. ii. 54). Successful lovers hardly need words, much less rant and cant. But Troilus goes further in his first dialogue with Cressida, which is, significantly, a dialogue in prose. 'Few words to fair faith' (III. ii. 94): so anxious is he to establish himself as the epitome of the 'plain and true' lover, that he damns as monstrous the usual lover's vows, with all their ludicrous rant and cant:

> *Troilus:* . . . in all Cupid's pageant there is presented no monster.
> *Cressida:* Nor nothing monstrous neither?
> *Troilus:* Nothing but our undertakings, when we vow to weep
> seas, live in fire, eat rocks, tame tigers.   (III. ii. 73–7)

[1] Schmidt di Simoni, p. 24.

It is typical of Cressida's comparative shallowness as a lover that she should almost immediately mistake Troilus's silence, which lasts while she 'blabs' of her feelings:

> See, see, your silence
> Cunning in dumbness, from my weakness draws
> My very soul of counsel.   (III. ii. 131-3)

She thinks that she has put herself in the power of this silent man. But there is nothing cunning in Troilus's dumbness. He is known to Ulysses, through Aeneas, as

> Not yet mature, yet matchless-firm of word;
> Speaking in deeds and deedless in his tongue.
>   (IV. v. 97-8)

Superficially this Troilus appears a very different person from the Troilus who, on occasions when there are no deeds to speak with, will rant and storm. In the parting scenes, he still manifests his 'plain and true' character, though with an increasing verbosity. True, his reaction to the news that Cressida must leave Troy is, especially when contrasted with her hysterical rant, notably restrained:

> Is it so concluded?
> . . . .
> How my achievements mock me!
> I will go meet them.   (IV. ii. 66, 69-70)

Yet it is interesting to observe how, carried away by his fixed idea of truth, he actually lands himself in the logical and verbal untruth characteristic of rant:

> *Troilus:* Hear me, my love: be thou but true of heart—
> *Cressida:* I true! how now! what wicked deem is this?
> *Troilus:* Nay, we must use expostulation kindly,
>   For it is parting from us.
>   I speak not 'be thou true', as fearing thee,
>
> . . . .
> But 'be thou true' say I, to fashion in
> My sequent protestation.   (IV. iv. 58-62, 65-6)

In other words, 'be thou true' is merely a rhetorical flourish meant
to introduce Troilus's plan to make Cressida 'nightly visitation' in
the Greek camp; and again, when he repeats it, to introduce a
vivid contrast between his simple self and certain crafty 'others':

> I cannot sing,
> Nor heel the high lavolt, nor sweeten talk,
> Nor play at subtle games—fair virtues all,
> To which the Grecians are most prompt and pregnant.
>
> . . . .
>
> Whiles others fish with craft for great opinion,
> I with great truth catch mere simplicity;
> Whilst some with cunning gild their copper crowns,
> With truth and plainness I do wear mine bare.
>
> (IV. iv. 85–8, 103–6)

This eloquent and persuasive talk in favour of 'mere simplicity'
has its own literary history. Though it would be unfair to term
it a kind of cantless cant, or to summon 'honest Iago' in evidence,
this is certainly a highly sophisticated way of projecting sincerity.
Sidney is its expert, differentiating the inarticulate Astrophil, who
'never dranke of *Aganippe* well', from the fluent hyperbolists,
who are by implication less sincere. (*Astrophil and Stella*, no. 74).
Shakespeare himself repudiates the 'strained touches rhetoric can
lend' in favour of 'true plain words by thy true-telling friend'
(Sonnet, no. 82). He makes Henry V's wooing sound the more
genuine in that this uncourtly but well-meaning soldier professes
to have 'no cunning in protestation' (*Henry V*, V. ii. 147). By
contrast Bertram, as vociferous as he is dishonourable, earns his
rebuke from Diana:

> 'Tis not the many oaths that makes the truth,
> But the plain single vow that is vow'd true.
> (*All's Well that Ends Well*, IV. ii. 21–2)

In his portrait of Troilus 'plain and true' Shakespeare has not,
therefore, departed from recognizable Elizabethan love conventions. He has them much in mind. Indeed, with careful de-
liberation, he incorporates both his lovers into the rhetoric of
love poetry in the splendid troth-plighting episode, where,

time suspended, they make themselves 'the bases of automatic similes':[1]

> True swains in love shall in the world to come
> Approve their truths by Troilus. When their rhymes,
> Full of protest, of oath, and big compare,
> Want similes, truth tired with iteration—
> 'As true as steel, as plantage to the moon,
> As sun to day, as turtle to her mate,
> As iron to adamant, as earth to th' centre'—
> Yet, after all comparisons of truth,
> As truth's authentic author to be cited,
> 'As true as Troilus' shall crown up the verse
> And sanctify the numbers.   (III. ii. 172–82)

'Full of protest, of oath, and big compare': the words bring a distinct reminder of the comic cant of fancy-mongers. In this scene Pandarus, too, preserves the comic tone amidst the splendour, as with a heavy bump he brings the transcendental lovers down to the here and now:

> Pandarus: Say 'amen'.
> Troilus: Amen.
> Cressida: Amen.
> Pandarus: Amen. Whereupon I will show you a chamber with
>   a bed.   (III. ii. 203–7)

'O withered truth' (V. ii. 47): Cressida's destruction of Troilus's ideal, banishing the spirit of comedy, also transforms his idiom again. The process begins in the scene of his disillusion, where Ulysses and Thersites watch him, as he watches her, flirting with Diomedes outside the tent of the traitor Calchas. This is peculiarly tense because what would be a full spate of rant is choked back by the situation and the onlookers:

> Troilus: O plague and madness!
> Ulysses: You are moved, prince; let us depart, I pray you,
>   Lest your displeasure should enlarge itself
>   To wrathful terms. This place is dangerous;
>   The time right deadly; I beseech you, go.

---

[1] Kimbrough, p. 75.

Troilus: Behold, I pray you!
Ulysses: Nay, good my lord, go off;
  You flow to great distraction; come, my lord.
  . . . .
Troilus: I pray you, stay; by hell and all hell's torments
  I will not speak a word.   (V. ii. 36–42, 44–5)

It is slow to break free even when Cressida and Diomedes have
departed. For, at first, Troilus's tirade on Cressida's unfaithfulness
is blocked by Thersites's sneer:

Troilus: Let it not be believed for womanhood!
  Think we had mothers . . .
Ulysses: What hath she done, prince, that can soil our
      mothers?
Troilus: Nothing at all, unless that this were she.
Thersites: Will a' swagger himself out on's own eyes?
                               (V. ii. 129–30, 134–6)

With Thersites replacing Pandarus as unofficial commentator on
the progress of Troilus's love affair, the tone inevitably becomes
more critical. Through his eyes the hero is seen as a swaggerer or
blusterer, who refuses to believe the evidence of his senses.

The transformation of Troilus's idiom is complete when he
enunciates a hatred of Diomedes equal to his love for Cressida:

> Not the dreadful spout
> Which shipmen do the hurricano call,
> Constringed in a mass by the almighty sun,
> Shall dizzy with more clamour Neptune's ear
> In his descent, than shall my prompted sword
> Falling on Diomed. (V. ii. 171–6)

Henceforward he is nothing but a passionate and terrible ranter
who continues to provoke disgust, alarm or dismay. 'Fie, savage,
fie!' is the chivalrous Hector's reaction to his furious speech:

> The venomed vengeance ride upon our swords,
> Spur them to ruthful work, rein them from ruth.
>   (V. iii. 47–8)

'My lord, you do discomfort all the host' is Aeneas's apt rebuke on hearing him agonize over Hector's death:

> Frown on, you heavens, effect your rage with speed!
> Sit, gods, upon your thrones and smite at Troy!
>
> (V. x. 7–8)

These notions are so exaggerated as to be misleading, and Troilus has therefore to re-explain his outlook in terms of vengeance:

> You vile abominable tents
> Thus proudly pight upon our Phrygian plains,
> Let Titan rise as early as he dare,
> I'll through and through you. (V. x. 23–6)

And, finally, Pandarus is left smarting under Troilus's whiplash:

> Hence, broker lackey! ignomy and shame
> Pursue thy life, and live aye with thy name! (V. x. 33–4)

Cressida's language, which contains far less rant and cant than Troilus's, is relevant here mainly as an offset to his. For, except in the troth-plighting, in a speech the exact rhetorical counterpart of his (III. ii. 182–95), she is practically never pitched in his key. In the first place her natural medium is lively, colloquial prose, so that there could hardly be a greater contrast between her entrée in the second scene and her lover's in the first. Thus, unlike Troilus, she plays Hamlet to Pandarus's Polonius, being wittier than both in, for example, the handling of comparison:

> *Pandarus:* Troilus is the better man of the two.
> *Cressida:* O Jupiter! there's no comparison.
> *Pandarus:* What, not between Troilus and Hector? Do you know a man if you see him?
> *Cressida:* Ay, if I ever saw him before and knew him.
> *Pandarus:* Well, I say Troilus is Troilus.
> *Cressida:* Then you say as I say; for I am sure he is not Hector.
>
> (I. ii. 59–66)

(Compare the ensuing exchange on the complexions of Troilus and Paris, 92 f.) In this long dialogue, Cressida's language is a means not of expressing but of disguising feeling. That she does, after all, love Troilus is not revealed till Pandarus has left:

But more in Troilus thousandfold I see
Than in the glass of Pandar's praise may be.
Yet hold I off: women are angels, wooing;
Things won are done—joy's soul lies in the doing.
That she beloved knows nought that knows not this:
Men prize the thing ungained more than it is.
That she was never yet that ever knew
Love got so sweet as when desire did sue.
Therefore this maxim out of love I teach:
'Achievement is command; ungained, beseech.'
(I. ii. 285–94)

There is a violent jolt in this shift to stiff couplets, which, however, still serve to maintain both the contrast with Troilus's fluent blank verse and the reserve Cressida intends. Reserve is too polite a word. Cressida's feminine technique of keeping a man on the boil by being hard to win is worthy of nothing superior to the third book of *Ars Amatoria*, and her devotion to it is shown by her remorseful repetition, much later, of the 'Yet hold I off' motif:

Prithee, tarry.
You men will never tarry.
O foolish Cressid! I might have still held off,
And then you would have tarried.   (IV. ii. 15–18)

Again, her glib generalizations, those 'maxims out of love', are a habit not to be discarded even in the moment of near commitment: 'They say all lovers swear more performance than they are able' etc. (III. ii. 83–4). Worst of all, those wooden couplets return to inhibit the expression of passion in her very last utterance:

Troilus, farewell! One eye yet looks on thee,
But with my heart the other eye doth see.
Ah, poor our sex! this fault in us I find,
The error of our eye directs our mind:
What error leads must err—O, then conclude
Minds swayed by eyes are full of turpitude.
(V. ii. 107–12)

Thersites's instantaneous paroyd—

> A proof of strength she could not publish more,
> Unless she said 'My mind is now turned whore.' (V. ii. 113–14)—

underlines the passionless platitudinousness of this manner of speaking.

Cressida lacks heart. At her first meeting with Troilus, she veers between 'holding off' and 'blabbing'. Aposiopesis is the natural rhetorical result of the fear of speaking out operating upon the pressure to do so:

> *Troilus:* O Cressida, how often have I wished me thus!
> *Cressida:* Wished, my lord? The gods grant—O, my lord!
> *Troilus:* What should they grant? What makes this pretty
> abruption?　　　　　　　　　　　　　　(III. ii. 60–5)

Immediately after the daring of a moment's surrender, when Cressida speaks out plain and true—

> Boldness comes to me now and brings me heart:
> Prince Troilus, I have loved you night and day
> For many weary months (112–14)—

another 'pretty abruption' signals renewed quailing:

> *Troilus:* Why was my Cressid then so hard to win?
> *Cressida:* Hard to seem won; but I was won, my lord,
> With the first glance that ever—pardon me. (115–17)

There follows intense regret—'Why have I blabbed?' (123)—with constant correction, modification or negation of what she says:

> In faith, I lie! . . . .
> . . . . Stop my mouth.
> . . . .
> My lord, I do beseech you, pardon me.
> 'Twas not my purpose thus to beg a kiss.
> 　　　　　　　　(120, 132, 135–6)

She even corrects the whole of her 'large confession', with the suggestion that it was not 'love' but 'craft'; that is, it was a trick to angle for Troilus's thoughts (152–54). Very different is Troilus's own form of rhetorical correction (epanorthosis), which is, naturally, a form of hyperbole:

And when fair Cressid comes into my thoughts—
So, traitor! 'When she comes!'—When is she thence?

(I. i. 32–3)

Cressida becomes a ranter, temporarily, at precisely the moment when Troilus is most restrained. When the news that she must leave Troy comes, she embarks on a routine of lamentation, invoking the gods, refusing to go, weeping, sobbing, threatening to tear her hair and scratch her cheeks (IV. ii. 84 f.). Her re-entry, after a short interval, shows her to be as great a sensualist in grief as Troilus is in love. Compare his anticipation of love—

> Th' imaginary relish is so sweet
> That it enchants my sense, etc. (III. ii. 18–19)—

with her response to Pandarus's plea for moderation:

> Why tell you me of moderation?
> The grief is fine, full, perfect, that I taste,
> And violenteth in a sense as strong
> As that which causeth it. How can I moderate it?
> If I could temporise with my affection,
> Or brew it to a weak and colder palate,
> The like allayment could I give my grief. (IV. iv. 2–8)

Both employ to good effect the play's predominant metaphor of tasting.[1] Both experience emotion as sensation, and therefore both transmute emotion into terms of sensation. Cressida's grief is, literally, sensational. And if this is psychologically convincing, it is also dramatically necessary. Cressida's immoderate expression of grief prepares for and emphasizes the depravity in her immediate desertion of Troilus. After this no one takes what she says seriously:

> O, these encounterers, so glib of tongue. (IV. ii. 58)

> And let your mind be coupled with your words. (V. ii. 16)

> Words, words, mere words; no matter from the heart.

(V. iii. 108)

---

[1] Caroline Spurgeon, *Shakespeare's Imagery* (Cambridge U. P., 1935), pp. 320–4, chart 7.

Men as different as Ulysses, Diomedes and Troilus are agreed in the final verdict on Cressida's 'words'.

'Sweet honey and sweet notes together fail' (V. x. 44): Pandarus's curtain speech, a comment on his own failure, also serves to dismiss the passionate rhetoric of love which Troilus has wasted upon so worthless a 'pearl' as Cressida. The passionate rhetoric of hate which has displaced it renders him no less sympathetic a character than he was before. Yet, ceasing to be a comic hero, Troilus has not become a tragic one. His exit leaves us aghast, 'Like wonder-wounded hearers', grateful even for such emotional refuge as the amiable but unedifying Pandarus is able to offer.

IV

Realism and Morality in
'Women Beware Women'

INGA-STINA EWBANK

In this essay I wish to examine the unity of Thomas Middleton's *Women Beware Women*. The art of this play is a compound of realism and morality—a compound which has laid the play open to some fundamental criticisms. Middleton has been praised for the naturalism and psychological insight of the first three and a half acts, and reprimanded for (allegedly) betraying his own vision and art by concluding the play in terms of conventional Jacobean morality and theatrical sensationalism.[1] Recent critics have, on the whole, abandoned T. S. Eliot's view of Middleton as a playwright who 'has no message; he is merely a great recorder';[2] and at the other extreme we have been given the 'highly moralistic artist who could skilfully pattern his actions in terms of a central theme'.[3] It seems to me that in *Women Beware Women* realism is not at war with morality; nor is one simply subservient to the other, like the two layers of an allegory. To understand their relationship one should, I think, look at the play through two (necessarily interrelated) questions: is there a unity of viewpoint? and, is there a dramatic unity?

I

'It isn't difficult to be a country gentleman's wife,' Rebecca thought. 'I think I could be a good woman if I had five

---

[1] See G. R. Hibbard, 'The Tragedies of Thomas Middleton and the Decadence of the Drama', *Renaissance and Modern Studies*, I (1957), esp. pp. 52–4; S. Schoenbaum, *Middleton's Tragedies* (N.Y., 1955), esp. p. 130; R. Ornstein, *The Moral Vision of Jacobean Tragedy* (Madison, 1960), esp. p. 191. There is an attempt to defend the play's conclusion in my essay on masques in plays, in *A Book of Masques. In Honour of Allardyce Nicoll* (Cambridge, 1967), pp. 445–7.

[2] 'Thomas Middleton', in *Selected Essays* (N.Y., 1950 edn.), p. 148.

[3] I. Ribner, 'Middleton's *Women Beware Women*: Poetic Imagery and the Moral Vision', *Tulane Studies in English*, IX (1959), 33.

thousand a year . . .' And who knows but Rebecca was right in
her speculations—and that it was only a question of money and
fortune which made the difference between her and an honest
woman? . . .

It may, perhaps, have struck her that to have been honest
and humble, to have done her duty, and to have marched
straightforward on her way, would have brought her as near
happiness as that path by which she was striving to attain it.
But . . . if ever Becky had these thoughts, she was accustomed
to walk round them, and not look in . . . ·

We grieve at being found out, and at the idea of shame or
punishment; but the mere sense of wrong makes very few
people unhappy in Vanity Fair.[1]

Middleton has often been seen as a seventeenth-century Ibsen,
but it might be more helpful to suggest that, if we were to look
for a nineteenth-century equivalent of *Women Beware Women*, we
would find it in the social novel. The themes of the play are
the favourite domestic and social ones of love, money and class—
indeed, G. R. Hibbard has spoken of *Women Beware Women* as
'the most powerful criticism of the education of women and of
the *mariage de convenance* in Elizabethan drama'.[2] The structure is
formed not so much by plot and subplot as by interlinked groups
of characters, so that the interest is spread over a cross-section
of society rather than being centred on the development of a few
characters. And, most important, Middleton's handling of the
moral perspective is, in its combination of apparent objectivity,
implicit evaluation and outright moralizing, curiously like that
of some nineteenth-century novelists.

The passage from *Vanity Fair* which I have quoted seems to me
in many ways a paradigm of the viewpoint of *Women Beware
Women*. Like *Vanity Fair*, *Women Beware Women* is a work without a hero (or heroine). Like Becky Sharp, all the characters in
the play confound the relation between money and honesty.
But it is the handling of the moral point-of-view which chiefly

[1] *Vanity Fair*, end of Chapter XLI.
[2] Hibbard, op. cit., p. 44.

makes this passage a parallel in narrative form to the dramatic art of *Women Beware Women*. Thackeray has the novelist's advantage —which he uses particularly fully in this novel[1]—of being able to illuminate his work 'by the author's own candles', but he does so in a variety of ways. First, Rebecca is given apparently free rein in the dialogue; then ('And who knows . . .') the author, with pretended objectivity, explains her in purely social-economic terms; then ('It may, perhaps, have struck her . . .') the omniscient observer becomes a moral judge of her actions; and finally his focus widens out to a universal moral statement, and to reveal the 'preacher in cap and bells'.

In much the same way Middleton deals with his characters in *Women Beware Women*. For most of the play, their own speeches are remarkably lacking in ethical insight into their own actions. There is a great deal of documentation provided, of a sociological rather than psychological nature, so that we may see how they have become what they are. Who knows but that Bianca and Leantio's marriage would have had a chance if they had been rich? Who knows but that Bianca, as she asks in her soliloquy in IV. i, would have been less easily corrupted, had she had a less restrained upbringing? Who knows but that Isabella would have been saved from incest, adultery and ultimately murder, but for the loveless and mercenary attitude of her father which has thrown her and Hippolito 'whole nights together in discourse' and leads to the miseries of enforced marriage with the Ward? This is not to say that Middleton, while making us ask these questions, remains the clinically detached observer, for throughout the play there is an undertow of reminders of an inexorable moral order. Many commentators have drawn attention to the persistent imagery of love/money, and love/gluttony, which interprets and judges the corruption of the play's world.[2] But the characters are kept away from comprehension of the moral order, even while

[1] There is an interesting discussion of this point in Kathleen Tillotson's, *Novels of the Eighteen-Forties* (Oxford, 1954): see the chapter on *Vanity Fair*.

[2] See especially M. C. Bradbrook, *Themes and Conventions of Elizabethan Tragedy* (Cambridge, 1935), Chapter IX; Ribner, op. cit.; and also Christopher Ricks's illuminating essay on 'Word-Play in *Women Beware Women*', R.E.S., n.s. XII (1961), 238–50.

E

referring to it, just as Becky Sharp uses the word 'good' without knowing what it means. Middleton manages this in several different ways. In the opening scene, Leantio delivers a diatribe against adultery:

> Methinks it should strike earthquakes in adulterers,
> When ev'n the very sheets they commit sin in,
> May prove, for aught they know, all their last garments.
>   (I. i. 22–4)[1]

which, on the face of it, has a Vendice-like vigour. But it is undercut by his own blatant Pharisaism:

> Now when I go to church, I can pray handsomely,

much as his speech, in III. i, on 'a glorious dangerous strumpet' is undercut by being in praise of this smug youth's sexual self-control. It is undercut, too, by searing irony, for when Leantio self-rightously proclaims

> I find no wish in me bent sinfully
> To this man's sister, or to that man's wife: (I. i. 28–9)

he is in fact unwittingly telling us exactly what is going to happen to sisters, brothers, men and wives, in the rest of the play. Such counterpointing (of the blindness of a character with generally valid judgments) is, however, dramatically uneconomic—hence the wordiness and drag of the opening scene. More successful is Middleton's technique of making his characters themselves thwart our ethical expectations. Hippolito, for example, first tells of his incestuous desires in a speech which, from its tense beginning, we might have expected to be one of inner struggle:

> I would 'twere fit to speak to her what I would, but
> 'Twas not a thing ordained; Heaven has forbid it.
>   (I. ii. 154–5)

---

[1] My quotations are from Roma Gill's edition of *Women Beware Women* in the New Mermaid series (London, 1968).

But it peters out into a clichéd resolution to stay silent—which he immediately proceeds to break. Finally, there is the technique of making the mercenary imagery invade what should be moral statements: so that in Livia's mock-sermon on incest even religion becomes a matter of economics:

> So he Heaven's bounty seems to scorn and mock,
> That spares free means, and spends of his own stock.
>
> (II. i. 15–16)

'Spatially', then, the play judges its characters throughout; but in terms of the time-sequence of the plot the Cardinal, with his explicit judgments in scenes i and ii of Act IV, becomes a wondrous necessary man. He is necessary because all the other characters, like Becky Sharp, 'walk round' such thoughts of sin as occur to them. His appearance corresponds to the omniscient judge stance in the Thackeray passage ('It may perhaps have struck her') and represents, to the play audience, a closing-in on the characters of the moral scheme they have ignored. And so, finally, that scheme is made explicit in action, in the moral retributions of the masque.

In terms of viewpoint, the masque corresponds to the generalization that concludes the Thackeray passage: as the characters are made to destroy themselves and each other with fiendish irony, the focus widens and the Cardinal becomes the preacher, left to point out what 'these ruins show too piteously'. The very deliberate contrivance of the ending, the patterning of the ironies:

> vengeance met vengeance
> Like a set match: as if the plagues of sin
> Had been agreed to meet here altogether, (V. ii. 155–7)

detach us and put us in the Cardinal's position. We see, too, that the moral view of the play is a question of the movement of the whole: rather than moral confusion, or inconsistency, there is a dynamism of viewpoint. This is where, ultimately, the dramatist scores over the novelist, for, because of the very nature of the form, his art is one of progression. In shaping his viewpoint, and so controlling our reactions, Middleton has used the art of drama to the full.

II

For, of course, *Women Beware Women* is supremely a work of the theatre. The strength of its dramatic poetry lies less in the obviously poetic speeches than in apparently unmemorable lines which are thrust into dramatic life through the context of character and action. Thus Isabella's words,

> In that small distance from yon man to me
> Lies sin enough to make a whole world perish,
>
> (IV. ii. 131–2)

which articulate the perverse horror of her situation, combining kinship and theatrical fact (for 'that small distance' is in blood as well as stage area) into what is virtually a metaphysical conceit, are in the theatre a far more powerful evocation of the reality of sin than any of the speeches of the Cardinal. Middleton's poetry is, to use Francis Fergusson's distinction,[1] more *of* the theatre than *in* it. It lies in the texture and the structure of his play, in the way social context is established, in the handling of characters and their relationships, and in the movement of the play as a whole. It is to these aspects of the play that I should now like to turn my attention.

One of the remarkable features of *Women Beware Women* is the realistic density of its *milieu*. Like no playwright outside Shakespeare, Middleton is able to give a solid context to his play world. It is partly a matter of his almost documentary use of objects—like Bianca's list of the furnishings lacking in Leantio's home, or the *two* handkerchiefs which the Mother runs to fetch in order to 'pocket up some sweetmeats' from the banquet. Partly it is a matter of scattering pieces of apparently irrelevant information—like the history of the room 'at the end of the dark parlour' where Leantio wants to immure Bianca, or of the genesis

[1] See his essay, '*Don Pimperlin*: Lorca's Theater-Poetry', *Kenyon Review*, XVII (1955), reprinted in *The Human Image in Dramatic Literature* (N.Y., Doubleday, 1957).

of the masque: prepared for the Duke's first wedding and can-
celled because of the death of Isabella's mother (a lady who, like
Leantio's father and Bianca's parents, is more present in the play
than the cast-list would suggest). These hints create a sense of
continuous life. How many husbands Livia has had *matters*, and
so does her story about the lady who, at the age of forty-nine,
kept a young 'friend'—who, in his turn,

> kept a quean or two with her own money,
> That robbed her of her plate and cut her throat.
> (II. ii. 165–6)

It is through carefully planted details like this little tragicomedy,
as well as through the action itself, that the quality of life in the
play is rendered.

One of the main sources of the density of *Women Beware
Women* is a type of metaphorical language which is common
throughout the play and used by all the characters, from the
Ward to the Cardinal. This is a simile, usually beginning 'as if'
or 'as when' and going on to draw an analogy between the
dramatic situation and another human situation. Thus, around
an already large group of characters, there is formed a whole
background cast, ranging, in the social spectrum, from the
country-maid 'dressing her head / By a dish of water' to 'great
gallants the next day / After revel'. Genre-paintings like the
Ward's reaction to kissing Isabella—'methinks it tasted as if a
man had stepped into a comfit-maker's shop to let a cart go by'
—are obviously an inheritance from Middleton's city-comedies;
but the technique as a whole is put to a specific use in the play. The
analogies which the characters are made to make so elaborately
tend, on the one hand, to play down and trivialize their emotions,
so as to suggest that they are composing satires on their own
experiences rather than coming to grips with them. Hippolito's
view of himself in the banquet scene,

> Like the mad misery of necessitous man,
> That parts from his good horse with many praises,
> And goes on foot himself, (III. ii. 199–201)

is an inept version of the emotions he should have—but is structurally apt as an anticipation of the following scene, in which Isabella is literally put through her paces before the Ward and Sordido. Leantio is constantly referring his experiences of love, for good or ill, to events in the life of 'some rich man', thus judging himself by the play's prevailing image-pattern of commercialized relationships. On the other hand, these analogies build up a dramatic metaphor of characters masquerading in other selves: selves which are parodies on human experience. This metaphor, which is a product of the play's realism as well as of its moral commentary, is also structural: it helps to prepare us for the masque which is the greatest masquerading, the climactic 'as if' image, of the play. No wonder, in a world where people so consistently relegate their experiences to some imaginary character, that Fabricio is confused about the identity of Livia's real and her masque self: 'I hope/*My sister Juno* has not served me so'.

Within the social context which Middleton so carefully establishes, the most outstanding 'figure in the carpet' is that of human relationships. For all T. S. Eliot's praise of Middleton's insight into the psychology of a few great individuals, the dramatic impact of *Women Beware Women* is made not so much through single characters—who are often static, or who, when like Bianca they change, are treated very much in dramatic shorthand—as through the dynamism of relationships. It is significant that Leantio, who has more and longer soliloquies than anyone else in the play, gives far less sense of an inner life than many of the other characters; and that he only really comes alive when he and Bianca, in IV. i, are pitted against each other in their new corruption and new finery. From the opening lines, where the Mother (who has no other name than 'Mother', or 'Widow') expounds the most intimate of all ties:

> Welcome, with all the affection of a mother,
> That comfort can express from natural love

to Fabricio's outcry:

> Dead? my girl dead? I hope
> My sister Juno has not served me so, (V. ii. 142–3)

the dramatic mechanism is a pattern of family relationships, confounded and criss-crossed by erotic links. The ordinary appellations of kinship are used with more than ordinary care and point—for example in Livia's scenes with her two brothers, or in the Mother's little ritual of the two kisses with which she moves from a 'gentlewoman' to a 'daughter' relationship with Bianca—and as relationships tangle so these words are fed with peculiar significance. There is pathos as well as irony in Isabella's appeals to her 'sweet uncle' when we know that his feeling for her is 'somewhat too unkindly' and that he loves her 'dearlier than an uncle can'; and Guardiano's shrewdness about other relationships makes his words to the Ward doubly ironic when he explains that

> he that weds her
> Marries her uncle's heart too. (III. ii. 18–19)

The reverberations of the action can make simple lines extremely sinister, as in Guardiano's gloating, Pandar-like greeting:

> How now, ward and nephew,
> Gentlewoman and niece! speak, is it so or not?
> (III. iii. 130–1)

And in the end, the conjunction of kinship words can produce an effect like oxymoron, as when the Duke asks Hippolito:

> How does that lusty widow, thy kind sister? (IV. i. 141)

The action of the play is a progressive perversion of natural relationships, one violation of a natural bond leading to another —as Leantio sees in a moralistic speech which anticipates the symmetry of retribution in the masque:

> Oh equal justice, thou hast met my sin
> With a full weight; I'm rightly now oppressed:
> All her [Bianca's] friends' heavy hearts lie in my breast.
> (III. ii. 97–9)

Livia, the king-pin of the *liaisons dangereuses* in the play, is, of course, the centre of these perversions. She forgets words of kinship when she sees people as touchstones against which to sharpen her wit (then both Fabricio and Hippolito become just 'man'); and she tramples on their meaning when it comes to a game of sexual intrigue:

> y'have few sisters
> That love their brother's ease 'bove their own honesties.
>   (II. i. 70–1)

In the scenes where she presides, complete havoc is played with family bonds; and well may she remind Isabella, after she has slandered 'your dead mother, my most loving sister' and set the niece on the way to an incestuous union:

> I pray forget not but to call me aunt still. (II. i. 167)

There is an ironic echo of this line in Isabella's recognition speech, perhaps the most sinister expression of what relationships have come to mean in the play:

> I'ld fain bring
> Her name no nearer to my blood than woman,
> And 'tis too much of that.   (IV. ii. 127–9)

Under the impact of this pervading dramatic image, the masque at the end becomes an integral part of the figure in the carpet. It has been defended, when at all, as a moral ritual 'utterly without logic in terms of human probability'.[1] Certainly, in real life, no people would plot so heedlessly against each other, or be subject to such coincidences. But within the play's own world, 'human probability' has come to mean the utter perversion of blood relationships; and so it seems logical enough that in conclusion an

---

[1] Ribner, op. cit. p. 33. The best discussion of the dramatic construction of the masque scene is, I think, R. B. Parker's, in 'Middleton's Experiments with Comedy and Judgement', *Jacobean Theatre*, *Stratford-upon-Avon Studies I*, ed. J. R. Brown and B. A. Harris (London, 1960), though I do not altogether agree with his comments on the emotional effect of the scene.

aunt should kill her niece, a niece her aunt, a sister her brother—
and, a fitting irony, that in her own masque Bianca should kill the
wrong brother. The context of the play makes us accept it, much
as we accept the spontaneous combustion in *Bleak House*: in terms
not of realism in the ordinary sense but of the reality of the central
image, which is one of self-destructiveness.

Destructiveness, of self and others, is also the ultimate effect
of the wit which is such an outstanding feature of the social
world of the play—wit in language and in action. 'It's a witty
age', Guardiano gloats after he has assisted in the seduction of
Bianca; and Livia is forever priding herself on her wit, from the
harmless 'I think I am more than witty. How think you, sir?', to
the more sinister:

> Sir, I could give as shrewd a lift to chastity
> As any she that wears a tongue in Florence:
> Sh'ad need be a good horsewoman and sit fast
> Whom my strong argument could not fling at last.
> (II. i. 36–9)

Wit in the play, as in this speech, means control of language as
well as situation—that is, of other people. Leantio is bought by
Livia, and Livia, who, when she first set eyes on Leantio, declared
herself 'dumb to any language now/ But love's', finds exactly the
right love's language for Leantio. Her analysis of marriage-for-
love puts in clear and persuasive terms what was an undertone in
Leantio's speeches in Act I:

> It brings on want, and want's the key of whoredom.
> I think y'had small means with her? (III. ii. 287–8)

And her direct offer to Leantio picks up his favourite term of
reference, the 'rich man':

> I have enough, sir,
> To make my friend a rich man in my life,
> A great man at my death. (III. ii. 362–4)

The way in which people's wit in the play is directed towards
using each other is epitomized in the clinching of their bargain:

> *Livia:* Do but you love enough, I'll give enough.
> *Leantio:* Troth then, I'll love enough and take enough.
> *Livia:* Then we are both pleased enough.   (III. ii. 376–8)

The chess scene is obviously the best example of wit in action
and language: double action and double talk. It shows, too, how,
as previously innocent characters are drawn into the whirlpool
of the play's sex-game, they join, as it were, the group language
and the group action. We learn how corruption has affected
Bianca through her single speech of outrage—'Now bless me from
a blasting!'—but, more sustainedly, through her new use of words.
In almost exactly the same terms as she spoke of Guardiano at
the outset of the scene, she now, with ironical doubleness, refers
to him as 'this kind, honest, courteous gentleman'; she makes
bawdy, albeit feeble, jokes in the banquet-scene and in the scenes
(IV. i) with the court ladies (this functions as an image of court-
wit) and with Leantio. And, of course, the ultimate product of
her wit is the masque she devises, fatal to the Duke and herself.

It has been well said that, throughout the play, Livia uses other
people like pawns in a game of chess;[1] but this is true for all the
other characters as well, even if they are not as clever at the game
as Livia. Guardiano plays on Fabricio, for Isabella; Fabricio uses
Isabella as a pawn in the monetary game; Isabella and Hippolito
use the Ward as 'the only veil wit can devise / To keep our acts
hid from sin-piercing eyes'; the Duke uses Hippolito to rid himself
and Bianca of Leantio. By the time death is involved as an element
in the game, only one outcome is possible; and, again, there is a
particular rightness about the masque, with its doubleness of
language and action, as the climactic and fatal game of this
society.

This is where, finally, the 'realism' of the masque scene lies.
In itself—even if there were not a long tradition of masques in
plays to support it—the masque is as natural a form of social

---

[1] Hibbard, op. cit., p. 50.

occasion in the world of the play as is the ball in *The Cherry Orchard* or the coffee-party in *Pillars of Society*. It is justified, too, by expectancies within the play itself, such as Leantio's image of how the idle rich live: 'Grow fat with ease, banquet, and toy and play.' It is set within a realistic framework of preparation, supplied by the scene between Guardiano and the Ward (V. i) and by Fabricio's bustling around with 'the model/ Of what's presented'. All this, together with Middleton's careful attention to the reaction of the masque audience, makes it a fully realized social occasion—as against the very schematic masques of, say, *The Revenger's Tragedy* and *Antonio's Revenge*.

But the 'realism' of the masque is also a matter of the structure of *Women Beware Women* as a whole. Middleton has a unique power of constructing group scenes, in which a very large number of people—virtually the whole cast—interact, take cues from each other, clash and score off each other. The three such scenes (if we may include the chess-scene, which in fact gradually involves nearly all the characters) form nodal points in the structure of the play. They form, too, a progression up the social scale. In the chess scene, Livia presides, and the Duke is hidden 'above'; in the banquet, the Duke presides, but the scene takes place in Livia's house; in the masque scene, the Duke presides, and the location is the Court. The structural irony of the masque is the ultimate involvement of all the characters in the masque. Bianca acts, in her aside, as a Presenter of her own private 'antimasque':

> But I have made surer work; . . .
> Cardinal, you die this night; the plot's laid surely:
> In time of sports death may steal in securely.
>   (V. ii. 17–22)

Soon she also has to act as an Epilogue:

> Pride, greatness, honours, beauty, youth, ambition—
> You must all down together; there's no help for't.
> Yet this my gladness is, that I remove,
> Tasting the same death in a cup of love.
>   (V. ii. 216–9)

The supposed audience become real masquers, just as in Livia's masque real death hits the masquers proper. The masque scene demonstrates in a stage image how the very ethos of their society has overtaken the characters. And, within this image we are prepared to accept that people speak their last words not as (psychological) characters but as masquers in the masque of retribution:

> *Hippolito:* Lust and forgetfulness has been amongst us,
>   And we are brought to nothing.

Critics have spoken of the coolness and detachment of this play which would seem to preclude a tragic vision. It is true that there is an extraordinary precision about the 'puppet show' at the end; but in the theatre, I think, our reaction is not all detachment. The masque scene shows Middleton's peculiar power of combining the ordinary with the horrible. As, in the chess scene, the ordinary surface of the game between Livia and the Mother is counterpointed with the horror of the act 'above', so, in the masque scene, the horror of the surface is placed in relation to the ordinary reactions of bystanders like Fabricio. The greatest emotional moments in the play are when a character gives voice to the tension between these two levels: Bianca's outcry at the evil she has seen 'above', or Fabricio's 'Dead? my girl dead? I hope / My sister Juno has not served me so'. Within Middleton's vision, as crystallized in these moments, there was room for a tragedy which not only dealt in conventional terms of retribution and damnation, but also saw the horror of life precisely in what men will do to men (or women to women). Therein, I think, lies Middleton's particular morality, as well as his realism; and as a theatrical image for this vision *Women Beware Women* has a unity of its own.

V

Sterne and Hume: A Bicentenary Essay

FRANCIS DOHERTY

WHEN Professor John Traugott links the names of Sterne and Hume by their mutual exploration of 'the difficulties inherent in Locke's rationalism', and suggests that Hume's praise of *Tristram Shandy* as 'the best book that has been writ by any Englishman these thirty years', he suggests a very provocative reason. Very possibly, Professor Traugott thinks, Hume saw how near the cleric from the enemy camp had come to his view.[1]

This view (which Professor Traugott establishes in a discussion of the central ethical doctrine of sympathy) would do something, one hopes, to qualify the more widely canvassed proposition that Sterne was simply Locke's disciple. My intention is more fully to pursue the hint, and come to some firmer conclusions about the nature of the relationship between the two contemporaries.

Everyone who reads Sterne knows very well that Locke's *Essay Concerning Human Understanding* is referred to as 'a history book . . . of what passes in a man's own mind',[2] that Sterne translates Locke into his own Shandean equivalents, especially when what is at stake is some opportunity to present sources of error and confusion in a man's mind. So, Locke's attack on the old scholastic philosophy in

> One may observe, in all languages, certain words, that, if they be examined, will be found, in their first original and their appropriated use, not to stand for any clear and distinct ideas. These, for the most part, the several sects of philosophy and religion have introduced. For their authors, or promoters, either affecting something singular and out of the way of

[1] *Tristram Shandy's World: Sterne's Philosophical Rhetoric* (University of California Press, 1954), p. 74.
[2] *The Life and Opinions of Tristram Shandy*, II, 2.

common apprehensions, or to support some strange opinions, or cover some weakness of their hypothesis, seldom fail to coin new words, and such as when they come to be examined, may justly be called insignificant terms.[1]

is turned into Shandy:

What a pudder and racket in COUNCILS about οὐσία and ὑπόστασις; and in the SCHOOLS of the learned about the power and about spirit—about essences, and about quintessences;—about substances, and about space.—What confusion in greater THEATRES from words of little meaning, and as indeterminate a sense.[2]

Such examples are too well-known to rehearse, but one might simply point out two facts about Locke's philosophical attitudes. First, that he was concerned to establish the boundaries of human knowledge:

Whereas, were the capacities of our understandings well considered, the extent of our knowledge discovered, and the horizon found, which sets the bounds between the enlightened and dark parts of things, between what is, and what is not comprehensible by us, men would perhaps with less scruple, acquiesce in the avowed ignorance of the one, and employ their thoughts and discourse with more advantage and satisfaction in the other.[3]

And, second, that he was at pains to establish the sources of error which arise out of man's attempt to communicate with other men, principally arising from the natural imperfection of language and from the individual character of ideas. In the act of communication, misunderstanding can arise because a word can suggest one idea to the first man and another entirely different to the next. This comes from the fact that ideas are personal and individual. The word stands for, is a sign of, the idea in the mind, and not anything in the external world. If the ideas men have are not identical then confusion will arise:

[1] *An Essay Concerning Human Understanding*, III, x, 1.
[2] *The Life and Opinions of Tristram Shandy*, II, 2.
[3] *An Essay Concerning Human Understanding*, I, i, 7.

And so in referring our ideas to those of other men, called, by the same names, ours may be false; and the idea in our minds which we express by the word *justice*, may perhaps be that which ought to have another name.[1]

This is the origin of the ambiguity which Sterne illustrates in Uncle Toby's mistake in thinking that his brother had enquired after his blister when he said 'ass'. Sterne sniggers but lays the blame on the thought that:

> our preconceptions having (you know) as great a power over the sounds of words as the shapes of things, he had imagined, that my father, who was not very ceremonious in his choice of words, had enquired after the part by its proper name.[2]

Possible ambiguity in words must be avoided, and Sterne continually states that it is not the word which is important, but the idea in the mind:

> ... 'tis one of the silliest things in one of them, to darken your hypothesis by placing a number, of tall, opake words, one before another, in a right line, betwixt your own and your reader's conception.[3]
>
> ... this comes, as all the world knows, from having half a dozen words for one thing; and so long, as what in this vessel of the human frame, is *Love*—may be *Hatred*, in that—*Sentiment* half a yard higher—and Nonsense . . .[4]

Because of the misunderstanding caused in the use of language Locke insisted upon men using no words:

> without a signification, no name without an idea for which he makes it stand.[5]

and upon definition of a term:

> where either common use has left it uncertain and loose (as

[1] Ibid., II, xxxii, 10.
[2] *The Life and Opinions of Tristram Shandy*, XIII, xxxii.
[3] Ibid., III, xx.
[4] Ibid., VIII, iv.
[5] *An Essay Concerning Human Understanding*, III, xi, 8.

it has in most names of very complex ideas) or where the term, being very material in the discourse, and that upon which it chiefly turns, is liable to any doubtfulness or mistake.[1]

This use of words with no signification is what Mr. Shandy accuses Trim of:

> I will enter into obligation this moment, said my father, to lay out all my aunt Dinah's legacy in charitable uses (of which, by the bye, my father had no high opinion), if the corporal has any one determinate idea annexed to any one word he has repeated.[2]

Locke found that there are certain things which human ignorance will never be able to know, such as the nature of substance, and consequently natural philosophy was not capable of being made a science.[3] But, although Locke recognizes certain boundaries to human knowledge and capacity, he does not have the same sense of man's ignorance that Sterne has. It is here that one senses the kinship of mind between Sterne and Hume.

To attempt an understanding of *Tristram Shandy*'s philosophical world simply in terms of Locke's *Essay* would be, in Shandean terms, to ride hobbyhorsically over the book, or, in Hume's terms:

> When a philosopher has once laid hold of a favourite principle, which perhaps accounts for many natural effects, he extends the same principle over the whole creation, and reduces it to every phenomenon, though by the most narrow and absurd reasoning.[4]

Far from denying, however, that reason and reasoning, and, in particular, 'narrow and absurd reasoning', plays a major part in *Tristram Shandy*, it would seem that the book demonstrates the limited place that reason has in human actions. The thought, in the end, would rhyme with that of Hume's brand of scepticism,

---

[1] Ibid., III, xi, 4.
[2] *The Life and Opinions of Tristram Shandy*, V, xxxii.
[3] *An Essay Concerning Human Understanding*, IV, iii, 26–31.
[4] 'The Sceptic', *Essays and Treatises on Several Subjects* (Edinburgh, 1793), Vol. I, p. 160.

that of the attempt 'to abate the Pride of *mere human Reasoners*, by showing them, that even with regard to Principles which seem the clearest, and which they are necessitated from the strongest Instincts of Nature to embrace, they are not able to attain a full Consistence and absolute Certainty'.[1]

And it is in Hume's essay, 'The Sceptic', that one sees one of the common links between the two men. Sterne would seem to be solely concerned with man's mind and its way of operating with its ideas, and not concerned with empirical truth. His concern with human behaviour and the behaviour of the mind would echo Hume's words in 'The Sceptic':

> The inference upon the whole is, that it is not from the value or worth of the object, which any person pursues, that we can determine his enjoyment, but merely from the passion with which he pursues it, and the success which he meets with in his pursuit. Objects have absolutely no worth or value in themselves. They derive their worth merely from the passion. If that is strong, and steady, and successful, the person is happy.[2]

Are we to consider that Uncle Toby's hobby-horse is a worse way of passing time than any other man's? As Traugott points out,[3] the activity of my uncle Toby might be seen in a larger satiric context:

> My father would often say to *Yoric*, that if any mortal in the whole universe had done such a thing, except his brother *Toby*, it would have been looked upon by the world as one of the most refined satyrs upon the parade and prancing manner, in which *Lewis* XIV from the beginning of the war, but particularly that very year, had taken the field—.[4]

We therefore have a complex situation, one where we are shown, via Walter, that a satire on 'parade and prancing' is a desirable thing, and yet the activity of Uncle Toby (seen by any observer

---

[1] *A Letter from a Gentleman to His Friend in Edinburgh*, (1745) (Edinburgh, 1967), p. 19.
[2] Op. cit., p. 168.
[3] *Tristram Shandy's World*, p. 74.
[4] *The Life and Opinions of Tristram Shandy*, VI, 22.

F

ignorant of Uncle Toby) would seem to be just that sort of 'refined
satyr' presented as a theatrical spectacle for the discerning. And,
despite this, Uncle Toby is safe from any such imputation, not
because he is a fool, but because he pursues his activity with no
thought beyond it; his passion is 'strong, steady and successful,
the person . . . happy'.

A different Sternean example is suggested by the continuation
of that quotation from Hume's essay, but it might seem possible to
argue for a much closer relationship:

> It cannot reasonably be doubted, but a little miss, dressed in a
> new gown for a dancing-school ball, receives as complete
> enjoyment as the greatest orator, who triumphs in the splendor
> of his eloquence, while he governs the passions and resolutions
> of a numerous assembly.[1]

This immediately sets 'gown' and 'eloquence' together so that
we are reminded very forcibly of Trim's oration in the kitchen
on the death of Bobby, and the ways we become aware of the
meaning of death for the audience, and, in particular, Susannah's
vision of the green gown. Sterne tells us to be aware of Locke on
the imperfections of words, but we are more aware of the closed
systems of minds operating with a publicly accepted, and publicly
understood language. Each mind's meaning is private; each
mind's speaking is public:

> —My young master in *London* is dead, said *Obadiah*.—A green
> sattin night-gown of my mother's, which had been twice
> scoured, was the first idea which *Obadiah*'s exclamation brought
> into *Susannah*'s head.—Well might *Locke* write a chapter upon
> the imperfections of words. —Then, quoth *Susannah*, we must
> all go into mourning.—But note a second time: the word
> *mourning*, notwithstanding *Susannah* made use of it herself—
> failed also of doing its office; it excited not one single idea,
> tinged either with grey or black,—all was green.—The green
> sattin night-gown hung there still.

For all the privacy of mental worlds, there is the ardour of
pursuit of the 'passion', which is self-justifying. The pursuit

[1] 'The Sceptic', op. cit., p. 168.

becomes frantic and kaleidoscopic, the outward behaviour conventionally solemn and quiescent:

> O! 'twill be the death of my poor mistress, cried *Susannah*.—My mother's whole wardrobe followed.—What a procession! her red damask,—her orange-tawny—her white and yellow lutestrings,—her brown taffata,—her bone-laced caps, her bed-gowns, and comfortable under-petticoats.—Not a rag was left behind.—'No,—*she will never look up again*,' said *Susannah*.

This is as interesting to the reader as it is to Sterne, as it is to Susannah; and her world, so simple, so radiant, contrasts finely with the eloquence of Trim, public orator controlling language and rousing emotions—the formula in Hume's essay:

> Are we not here now, continued the Corporal, (striking the end of his stick perpendicularly upon the floor, so as to give an idea of health and stability)—and are we not—(dropping his hat upon the ground) gone! in a moment!—'Twas infinitely striking! *Susannah* burst into a flood of tears.—We are not stocks and stones.—*Jonathan*, *Obadiah*, the cook-maid, all melted.—The foolish fat scullion herself, who was scouring a fish-kettle upon her knees, was rous'd with it.—The whole kitchen crouded about the corporal.[1]

We compare my father's combative eloquence which was hazardous to antagonists and Trim's which moves the hearers, and we see the difference possible for Sterne in two ways of looking at the orator, the Lockean self-deception, and the Humean self-satisfaction. This might help us rather better to see how Sterne can lay hold on different handles to lift his work out of the ordinary way, and, perhaps, to allow more puzzle and uncertainty to the reader.

The striking thing about the feel of Sterne's work is a sense of bewilderment and riddle, which is by no means part of Locke. Locke's purpose had been to limit the scope of human understanding, thereby to rid philosophy of error, and to fix the proper objects of human attainment and interest. Finding the limits in no way destroyed, for him, the faith in human understanding,

[1] *The Life and Opinions of Tristram Shandy*, V, vii.

provided only that it kept strictly within its bounds; nor did it warrant the bewilderment of Sterne. For Hume, our understanding is not the source of any certainty; the only certainty is that of concrete observable facts, and beyond that is darkness and mystery. Sterne frequently expressed his conviction that reality is enclosed in mystery and riddle. An examination of the human predicament leads to his quite serious assertion that

> we live among mysteries and riddles; and almost everything which comes in our way, in one light or other, may be said to baffle our understandings, yet seldom so as to mistake in extremities, and take one contrary for another . . .[1]

And Man himself is

> surely a compound of riddles and contradictions.[2]

It is not only in the Sermons that we find the serious, straight-faced, Sterne; the same thoughts echo in the novel:

> we live in a world beset on all sides with mysteries and riddles;[3]

and, more insistently:

> But mark, madam, we live amongst riddles and mysteries— the most obvious things, which come in our way, have dark sides, which the quickest sight cannot penetrate into; and even the clearest and most exalted understandings amongst us find ourselves puzzled and at a loss in almost every cranny of nature's works: so that this, like a thousand other things, falls but for us in a way, which tho' we cannot reason upon it—yet we find the good of it, may it please your reverences and your worships —and that's enough for us.[4]

Because Sterne felt so strongly the absurdities which are part of the fabric of life and of human nature, I feel that he was in tune with the scepticism of Hume, rather than with Locke's philosophy of limited understanding. This scepticism of both men grew out

[1] Sermon XIX, 'Felix's Behaviour Towards Paul Examined'.
[2] Sermon XX, 'The Prodigal Son'.
[3] *The Life and Opinions of Tristram Shandy*, IX, xxii.
[4] IV, xvii.

of Locke, but the end-result is not Lockean. For Hume, reason leads only to insoluble puzzles and absurdities:

> Yet still reason must remain restless, and unquiet, even with regard to that scepticism, to which she is driven by these seeming absurdities and contradictions. How any clear, distinct idea can contain circumstances, contradictory to itself, or to any other clear, distinct idea, is absolutely incomprehensible; and is, perhaps, as absurd as any proposition, which can be formed. So that nothing can be more sceptical, or more full of doubt and hesitation, than this scepticism itself, which arises from some of the paradoxical conclusions of geometry or the science of quantity.[1]

All honest philosophical thought leads to absurdity, confusion and doubt, but:

> . . . though a Pyrrhonian may throw himself or others into a momentary amazement and confusion by his profound reasonings; the first and most trivial event in life will put to flight all his doubts and scruples, and leave him the same, in every point of action and speculation, with the philosophers of every other sect, or with those who never concerned themselves in any philosophical researches. When he awakes from his dream, he will be the first to join in the laugh against himself, and to confess, that all his objections are mere amusement, and can have no other tendency than to show the whimsical condition of mankind, who must act and reason and believe; though they are not able, by their most diligent enquiry, to satisfy themselves concerning the foundation of these operations, or to remove the objections which may be raised against them.[2]

It is this final conclusion that we must consider as agreeing with Sterne's response. The evident absurdities which are in life are the reason for laughter, the laughter of scepticism. When Sterne laughs at the misfortunes of others and the incomprehensible, he laughs, as Voltaire did, to keep his sanity.

Granted that Sterne needed to laugh to keep alive and sane, there seems to be more in his laughter than its therapeutic value. It is

---

[1] *An Enquiry Concerning Human Understanding*, Section XII, Part II.
[2] Ibid.

an acknowledgement of scepticism to the incomprehensible. The incomprehensibility of events seems only equalled by the misfortunes which they bring. Nothing goes right for Tristram Shandy, the hero, and Mr. Shandy sums up the situation of man in his reflections:

> When I reflect, brother *Toby*, upon MAN; and take a view of that dark side of him which represents his life as open to many causes of trouble—when I consider, brother *Toby*, how oft we eat the bread of affliction, and that we are born to it, as to the portion of our inheritance—[1]

then Sterne's response is to laugh. We shall see more of his preoccupation with human misfortune later, some of the more specific influences of Hume must be considered now.

Ignorance and scepticism are the conclusions which Hume draws from every problem which he poses. He believed, unlike Locke, in the possibility of attaining to a science of natural philosophy, based solely upon the observation of empirical data:

> We must, therefore, glean up our experiments in this science from a cautious observation of human life, and take them as they appear in the common course of the world, by men's behaviour in company, in affairs, and in their pleasures. Where experiments of this kind are judiciously collected and compared, we may hope to establish on them a science which will not be inferior in certainty, and will be superior in utility, to any other of human comprehension.[2]

This stress on observation is greater in Hume than in Locke, while his denigration of metaphysics is substantially the same:

> Here indeed lies the justest and most plausible objection against a considerable part of metaphysics, that they are not properly a science; but arise either from the fruitless efforts of human vanity, which would penetrate into subjects utterly inaccessible to the understanding, or from the craft of popular superstitions, which, being unable to defend themselves on fair ground,

[1] *The Life and Opinions of Tristram Shandy*, IV, vii.
[2] *A Treatise of Human Nature*, Introduction.

raise these intangling brambles to cover and protest their weakness.[1]

For Sterne, too, the true philosopher was not the metaphysician, no matter how stimulating Mr. Shandy found his abstruse enquiries, but the man who observed; who, like Yorick,

> would both hear and see enough to keep his philosophy from rusting.[2]

The essential thing was to be in close, alive, contact with people and things, if one was to be a philosopher. Consequently, Hume says in the *Enquiry*:

> Hence likewise the benefit of that experience, acquired by long life and a variety of business and company, in order to instruct us in the principles of human nature, and regulate our future conduct as well as speculation. By means of this guide, we mount up to the knowledge of men's inclinations and motives, from their actions, expressions, and even gestures; and again descend to the interpretation of their actions from our knowledge of their motives and inclinations. The general observations treasured up by a course of experience, give us the clue of human nature, and teach us to unravel all its intricacies.[3]

This is why Sterne wanted to delineate his characters in such detail. His amateur achievements in painting have been suggested as the reason for his exquisite sense of 'tableau'; but, although these must have helped his powers of observation, the reason lies deeper. Sterne's reason is Hume's reason. Detail counts because it is that which, when observed carefully, gives the clue to the behaviour and character of men, human psychology.

Sterne and Hume can be placed firmly together by this stress on observation; both think that details are important as being the clues the philosopher, the student of human nature, must follow. This reliance upon data is the compensation for the ridicule heaped on the metaphysician, the man who relied only on reason. And Mr. Shandy stands as a ready exemplar:

[1] *Enquiry*, Section I.
[2] *The Life and Opinions of Tristram Shandy*, I, x.
[3] Section VIII, Part I.

... What a conjecture was here lost—My father in one of his best explanatory moods—in eager pursuit of a metaphysical point into the very regions, where clouds and thick darkness would soon have encompassed it about.[1]

Such is the *terminus ad quem* of the metaphysician's speculation.

Another metaphysical speculation, for Hume, was the current Eighteenth Century search in Nature of her 'hidden springs and principles'. In Section I of the *Enquiry* he asks the question:

> But may we not hope, that philosophy, if cultivated with care, and encouraged by the attention of the public, may carry its researches still farther, and discover, at least in some degree, the secret springs and principles, by which the human mind is actuated in its operations?

To seek to find principles beyond the concrete observable data available to an observer, and to rely upon human reason for this was, for him, a vain task:

> These ultimate springs and principles are totally shut up from human curiosity and enquiry. . . . The most perfect philosophy of the natural kind only staves off our ignorance a little longer: as perhaps the most perfect philosophy of the moral or metaphysical kind serves only to discover larger portions of it. Thus the observation of human blindness and weakness is the result of all philosophy, and meets us at every turn, in spite of our endeavours to elude or avoid it.[2]

This search for something behind observed events is mentioned by Sterne in *Tristram Shandy*:

> When great or unexpected events fall out upon the stage of this sublimary world—the mind of man, which is an inquisitive kind of substance, naturally takes a flight behind the scenes to see what is the cause and first spring of them,[3]

and again:

[1] *The Life and Opinions of Tristram Shandy*, III, ix.
[2] *Enquiry*, Section IV, Part I.
[3] *The Life and Opinions of Tristram Shandy*, IV, xxvii.

This requires a second translation:—it shows that little know-ledge is got by mere words—we must go up to the first springs.[1]

However, this use of a contemporary locution in Sterne is easily contrasted with what actually happens. This philosopher in his search for 'the first springs' is indulging in 'the dreams of philosophy',[2] and finds himself examining mysteries, insoluble puzzles, the 'dark sides' of things; he must turn for truth and intelligible propositions to actual events. He must be content to find truth from the detail attentively adverted to:

> Let no man say from what taggs and jaggs hints may not be cut out for the advancement of human knowledge.[3]

It is the trifle, the detail, the accident, that is important for the philosophic observer. Again and again Sterne witnesses the influ-ence on his thought of the discovery of the vastly important, but hardly noticeable incident:

> It is curious to observe the triumph of slight incidents over the mind:—what incredible weight they have in forming and governing our opinions, both of men and things—that trifles, light as air, shall waft a belief into the soul, and plant it immove-ably within us.[4]

The influence on action and behaviour is attested by the incident of Uncle Toby's Fly, where Sterne proclaims:

> this I know, that the lesson of universal good-will then taught and imprinted by my uncle *Toby*, has never since been worn out of my mind: And tho' I would not depreciate what the study of the *Literae humaniores*, at the university, have done for me in that respect, or discredit the other helps of an expensive education bestowed on me, both at home and abroad since; —yet I often think that I owe one half of my philanthropy to that one accidental impression.[5]

[1] Ibid., IV, xx.
[2] Ibid., IV, xxvii.
[3] Ibid., VI, xxvi.
[4] Ibid., IV, xxvii.
[5] Ibid., II, xii.

Another feature of Sterne's thought which was undoubtedly influenced by Hume is the doctrine of the association of ideas. Rather than following Locke in seeing the association of ideas as a form of madness,[1] it is more likely that Sterne followed Hume in their common view of the central positioning of this principle of human thinking.

David Hume accorded to it the operancy and force, even necessity, of the law of gravity. It was a psychological reality, and by no means an aberration:

> Here is a kind of ATTRACTION, which in the mental world will be found to have as extraordinary effects as in the natural, and to show itself in as many and as varied forms.[2]

Like the force of gravity this principle for Hume was ultimate and evident.

Sterne consciously organized his work upon the principle of the association of ideas, which could always be called upon to explain all the twists and turns of his writing, the 'rash jerks and hair-brained quirks'. Chapter XIX of Book VII of *Tristram Shandy* illustrates this and gives Sterne's own acknowledgment of it:

> In mentioning the word *gay* (as in the close of the last chapter) it puts one (i.e. an author) in mind of the word *spleen*—especially if he has anything to say upon it: not that by any analysis—or that from any table of interest or genealogy, there appears much more ground of alliance betwixt them, than betwixt light and darkness, or any two of the most unfriendly opposites in nature—only 'tis an undercraft of authors to keep up a good understanding amongst words, as politicians do amongst men —not knowing how near they may be under a necessity of placing them to each other.

In a note to *Enquiry*, Section III, Hume treats *contrast* as an example of the association of ideas:

> Contrast or contrariety is also a connexion among ideas: but it may, perhaps, be considered as a mixture of *causation* and

---

[1] *An Essay Concerning Human Understanding*, II, xxxiii, 4.
[2] *Treatise*, Book I, Part I, iv.

resemblance. When two objects are contrary, the one destroys the other; that is, the cause of its annihilation, and the idea of the annihilation of an object implies the idea of its former existence.

The aptness of Sterne's example is an indication that the 'ground of alliance' he speaks of is remarkably like Hume's thought and writing upon the 'principles of association'; as Hume himself said:

> I do not find that any philosopher has attempted to ennumerate or class all the principles of association; a subject however, that seems worthy of curiosity.[1]

Sterne had evidently thought about association in a similar way to Hume, and insisted upon its power over us, which might seem irrational, but was a fact which had to be admitted. If this principle of association is irrational, then rational life contains this element of irrationality and Sterne would say:

> how little we truly know of ourselves.[2]

Tristram's inordinate longing to see the tomb of the lovers is a case in point, and he exclaims:

> I never could get into a scrape of that kind in my life, but this *tomb of the lovers* would, somehow or other, come in at the close —nay such a kind of empire had it establish'd over me, that I could seldom think or speak of *Lyons*—and sometimes not so much as see even a *Lyons-wastcoat*, but this remnant of antiquity would present itself to my fancy.[3]

The kind of empire might be irrational and inconvenient, but natural and unavoidable; many of our actions are, for Sterne, based upon this same principle which by-passes rational judgment. In *A Sentimental Journey* Yorick buys a set of Shakespeare's works, not from conscious choice, but as the result of a chain of associations produced by a chance remark of an old French officer:

> What the old French officer had delivered upon travelling,

[1] *Enquiry,* Section III.
[2] Sermon IV, 'Self Knowledge'.
[3] *The Life and Opinions of Tristram Shandy,* VII, xxxi.

bringing Polonius's advice to his son upon the same subject into my head, and that bringing in Hamlet; and Hamlet the rest of Shakespeare's works, I stopp'd at the Quai de Conti in my return home, to purchase the whole set.[1]

So much of life depends on this principle, and all the advice given to the *fille de chambre* was lost if Yorick had not used the Principle:

> My advice, my dear, would not have been worth a pin to you, said I, if I had not given this along with it: but now, when you see the crown, you'll remember it, so don't, my dear, lay it out in ribbands.[1]

This dependence upon the principle of the association of ideas would seem to set Sterne more nearly in the philosophic thought of his contemporary, Hume, than in that of his alleged master, Locke. Hume, in the *Abstract of a Treatise of Human Nature*, says of himself, as a philosopher:

> but if anything can entitle the author to so glorious a name as that of an *inventor*, it is the use he makes of the principle of the association of ideas, which enters into most of his philosophy. Our imagination has a great authority over our ideas; and there are no ideas that are different from each other which it cannot separate, and join, and compose into all the varieties of fiction.

From being an almost incidental issue in Locke's philosophy (actually a postscript), and then only as being an explanation of abnormal behaviour, the association of ideas was made basic to the understanding of the mechanics of thought by Hume. He did not deny that this principle can be the source of error by a wrong association of ideas, but rather that

> Were ideas entirely loose and unconnected, chance alone would join them; and it is impossible the same simple ideas should fall regularly into complex ones (as they commonly do), without some bond of union among them, some association quality by which one idea naturally introduces another.[2]

This more common-sense view is shared by Sterne. While

---

[1] *A Sentimental Journey*, 'The Fille de Chambre: Paris'.
[2] *A Treatise of Human Nature*, Book I, Part I, iv.

organizing *Tristram Shandy* on this principle, he does not lose sight of the infinite fun to be derived from wrong associations. Uncle Toby is often a prime offender and Susannah's head seems to be one that is incapable of having any but wrong associations, and so it goes on.

The important thing seems to be that Sterne tells us when someone is misusing the association principle, therefore indicating that it is not always used in this way; there is a normal function. Quite definitely he is at one with Hume, and in disagreement with Locke.

Both sceptical philosopher and clerical novelist agree in the end that the function of their differing (but oddly similar) creative efforts is a self-regarding and self-fulfilling one: a hobby-horse. In a word, says Hume—and Sterne thinks the same—

In a word, human life is more governed by fortune than by reason; is to be regarded more as a dull pastime than as a serious occupation; and is more influenced by particular humour than by general principles . . . Even to reason so carefully concerning it, and to fix with accuracy its just idea, would be overvaluing it, were it not that to some tempers this occupation is one of the most amusing in which life could possibly be employed.[1]

[1] 'The Sceptic', op. cit., p. 182.

VI

Poetry and the Arts

G. WILSON KNIGHT

The art of writing, said Conrad in his preface to *The Nigger of the Narcissus*, 'must strenuously aspire to the plasticity of sculpture, to the colour of painting, and to the magic suggestiveness of music'. In epic, drama, and the novel affairs and energies are given design and rhythm; in lyric, personal emotions are expressed by song, melody and rhyme. Sometimes poetry of weight deliberately takes the other arts as its subject, often in contrast with nature, and in so doing makes valuable commentaries on them, on itself, and on the meanings of existence. Whether in literature or in life it will be found that the separation of the spatial and the temporal, of sight and sound, is provisional only, and often dangerous, whereas the aim must always be a fusion. Life exists in space-time, and space-time may often be equated with eternity. Symbols of eternity must have conviction and weight; but if too heavily used, or too rigidly demarked from organic life, they lose authority.

These remarks may serve as an introduction to some remarks on certain poems of Tennyson, Browning, O'Shaughnessy and Yeats.

In writing of Milton's style in my recent *Poets of Action* (in an essay originally published in *The Burning Oracle*), I showed how his attempt to impose eternal significances on his material by too heavy a stress on solidifications, too insistent a reliance on design and artefact, could, except when a supreme event were being treated, become constricting. In my *Laureate of Peace* the exquisitely handled spatial arts of Pope's *Temple of Fame* were contrasted with the more directly human concern of his other poetry. *The Starlit Dome* explored the pervasive use of domes and other architectural, usually sacred, structures in balance with nature throughout the Romantics, finding *Kubla Khan* to be a key-poem and Keats's peculiar excellence to be a perfect fusion, moment by moment, of the fluid and the solid, of nature and art. In Wordsworth's later poetry the use of architecture is excessive; and indeed the dome-symbol itself may, if used with too recurring a facility, constitute a temptation and a danger.[1]

Both Tennyson and Browning have left us interesting critiques of what Nietzsche called the 'Apollonian' arts of spatial design. In them they suspect, as he did, the will to tidy up and control the disconcerting mysteries and energies of existence; and certainly when poetry relies on them the eternity symbolized may be too easily depicted; may be, as it were, claimed without having been properly re-created. Such symbols lure the poet from the far more arduous task of creating *structure* and *form* from the complications and turmoils of human existence, whilst offering a too-easy insight parasitic on another art.

This is the theme of Tennyson's *Palace of Art*. The poet recounts how he made for himself 'a lordly pleasure-house' set high on rock, with wonderful lawns and artefacts of all sorts; living fountains, cloisters 'branch'd like mighty woods', windows that burned with 'slow-flaming crimson fires', each room carefully devised 'from living Nature'. There are numerous pictures on tapestry showing various actions: the hunter with 'puff'd cheek' blowing his horn, a roaring sea which you can almost hear, reapers at their labour, a smiling Virgin with her Child, St. Cecily in sleep over-watched by an angel, houris awaiting 'the dying Islamite', Arthur asleep in Avalon,

> Or hollowing one hand against his ear,
> To list a foot-fall, ere he saw
> The wood-nymph, stay'd the Ausonian king to hear
> Of wisdom and of law.

There is music too, great bells which 'moved of themselves with silver sound', and portraits of great poets, Milton, Shakespeare, Dante, Homer. The floor is a mosaic illustrating 'cycles of the human tale'. The arches 'lift' themselves 'up'—it is all, as in

[1] Byron's use of the spatial arts is entangled in his prevailing humanism and sense of energies. See my *Byron and Shakespeare*, 48–50; and my discussion throughout of *Don Juan* in *Poets of Action*

Pope's *Temple of Fame, living*—and it seems that angels rise and descend from on high, bringing and taking gifts. There is the inevitable statuary:

> And high on every peak a statue seem'd
> To hang on tip-toe, tossing up
> A cloud of incense of all odour steam'd
> From out a golden cup.

In this elevated retreat the poet's soul sings, accompanied by the great and wise of all ages and enjoying a god-like isolation.

Though our description emphasizes at every point the living and moving qualities of the designs, yet the retreat is parasitic on the visual arts or antecedent works of great poetry. It represents an Apollonian contemplation and contentment with no engagement of the Dionysian, the basic energies, the raw material of human nature. We are next shown how the severance from humankind, here regarded by the superior poet as little better than beasts, raises demons in the depths of his own personality. Ghosts, nightmares, and uttermost melancholia and neurosis assail and agonize him; and we are made by a succession of poignant stanzas to feel that such a retreat is suicidal. This recognized, the solution is simple: to descend again to mankind, and will to lift them to his palace.

The poem is important not only as a key to Tennyson's later work,[1] but as marking a necessary choice, a diverging of the ways, to be faced by all poets; indeed by all men. Not only Renaissance poetry, but life itself, can be discussed in these terms.

In his *Allegory of Love* (VII. iii) C. S. Lewis contrasted Spenser's Bower of Bliss and Garden of Adonis; the one a place of enervate sensuousness and mental artistry, the other of movement, dance and creation. Such are the dangers of relaxation; at its worst, the sluggard self-enjoyment of Tennyson's Lotus Eaters; at its best, of what Nietzsche calls the 'pure' or 'will-less' contemplation of Apollonian pictures (*The Birth of Tragedy*, V, XXII); of art-for-art's sake; of idolatry. Above all, there is the danger of

---

[1] For my brief acount of Tennyson's weightier poetry see *The Times Literary Supplement*, 10 Oct., 1942; reprinted in *Hiroshima* (1946; II. iv).

failing to live, or write, from the vital, human, centres; the denial
of nature's, which are, as Pope tells us, the divine, energies.

No one believed in those energies more firmly than Browning,
who ranks high among our poetic humanists. No poet had more
right than he to name a volume *Men and Women*; indeed, he offers
exactly what the Romantics, apart from Byron, lacked, while
lacking what they offer. Browning gives us humanity with com-
paratively little emphasis on either nature, except for fire and
the heavenly bodies,[1] or the transcendent, except in so far as it
can be felt to flower from human instincts, passions and purposes.
His human projection is nevertheless one of abundant resource
and interest. The emphasis is equally physical and spiritual,
specifically concentrating on a just balance, as when in *Rabbi
Ben Ezra* he sees man in his temporal existence as a 'cup' being
moulded by the Potter's artistry into a 'whole' of which age is as
important a constituent as the physical 'rose-mesh' of youth. Life
in time is creating an entity, a completed solid, made for use in
another dimension:

> Look not thou down but up!
> To uses of a cup,
> The festal board, lamp's flash and trumpet's peal,
> The new wine's foaming flow,
> The Master's lips a-glow!
> Thou, Heaven's consummate cup, what need'st
> thou with earth's wheel?

Perhaps in no other poem do we see more clearly how well the
super-temporal may be approached in terms of plastic art, provided always that distinctions are not too rigid and vitality be
preserved. The 'clay' here is bodily life; the Potter's wheel 'spins
fast', impressing a still circularity on temporal motion; the whole
cup, from birth to death, is made; then, and only then, is its true
purpose realized, in festal splendour.

Two of Browning's dramatic monologues concerning painters
are peculiarly revealing. In *Andrea del Sarto* we have a painter of

---

[1] See *Browning's Star Imagery*, C. Willard Smith (Princeton University Press,
1941).

assured technique who nevertheless knows that he has never properly expressed that urgent inner life that is the 'soul'. His work
is perfected, but static, and lesser artists have more of the real thing :

> There burns a truer light of God in them,
> In their vexed beating, stuffed and stopped-up brain,
> Heart, or whate'er else, than goes on to prompt
> This low-pulsed forthright craftsman's hand of mine . . .

His art, as art, may be higher than theirs; but, by reason of its
very perfection, because his 'reach' does not exceed his 'grasp', he,
as a man, is not orientated towards the reality of 'heaven'. In our
other monologue *Fra Lippo Lippi*, we meet an artist who, urged
to paint pictures that incite men to devotion rather than any
interest in the human form, defends the rights of the body while
insisting that the spiritual will be only of value if flowering from
the physical. We can feel Browning fighting for physical reality
and vitality as against a premature spiritualizing of the human.
The two monologues make a single emphasis.

Browning emphasizes the value of effort, of striving, of the
indomitable will to accomplish more than is, in fact, possible.
From the vital centres alone, as Pope too insists, can any real virtue,
in art or life, blossom. *The Statue and the Bust* is accordingly a
central poem.

The Great-Duke Ferdinand loves a lady prisoned in a palace at
Florence and married to a stern man; and she returns his love. Both
plan to elope, but, Hamlet-like, they put off the action day by day:

> But next day passed, and next day yet,
> With still fresh cause to wait one day more
> Ere each leaped over the parapet.

Originally the Duke had planned to win his 'cup of bliss', whatever its cost 'to body or soul'; but worldly wisdom intrudes, for,
after all, 'the world and its ways have a certain worth'. Day by
day the Duke rides through the square and sees his lady at the
window; and she returns his gaze; and that is all. But at last the
lovers begin to age, and so the lady asks her attendants to summon
a skilful sculptor,

> Who fashions the clay no love will change,
> And fixes a beauty never to fade.

She has her bust set in the window to perpetuate her love 'waiting as ever, mute the while'. After death, it will, ironically, prove a solace, since

> I did no more while my heart was warm
> Than does that image, my pale-faced friend.

Similarly, the Duke has his statue placed in the square, done on horseback to the life, 'as the crafty sculptor can', 'brave in bronze'. Their romance is thus perpetuated; and in their remaining content with such a perpetuation lies their condemnation.

Life has passed them by. True, the proposed act was a sin, but the poet explicitly asserts that his statement exists below, or above, moral distinction:

> I hear you reproach, 'But delay was best,
> For their end was a crime'—Oh, a crime will do
> As well, I reply, to serve for a test.

The doctrine is a doctrine of perpetual striving:

> Let a man contend to the uttermost
> For his life's set prize, be it what it will!

If virtue be the argument, what virtue *is* virtue without such striving, such inner energy, as the prerequisite? Such was the virtue of the 'soldier-saints' who 'burn upward each to his point of bliss'; and such virtue the parable negatively defines. It is interesting to observe how the rejection of life and its opportunities is here related to the extreme Apollonianism—in Nietzsche's terms—of sculpture. We may recall the different reference of Hamlet's not dissimilar problem to the more dynamic art of acting: 'Is it not monstrous that this player here . . .' (*Hamlet*, II. ii. 577).

Browning knows well enough the excellences of painting, and in *Pippa Passes* (II) he has given us a remarkable passage on the sculptor's art, showing both a keen technical understanding and a sense of the spiritual powers at play. But he can nevertheless emphasize the inadequacy not only of any art, but of all the arts together.

The thought is developed in *Cleon*, an epistle from the poet and artist, Cleon, to a king, Protus. Cleon is a practitioner in various arts and a connoisseur of them all: poetry, song, sculpture, painting, music and philosophy. He is one in whom all the best of Hellenic paganism appears to be consummated. Rationally, he has reason for pride. He claims for himself no supreme excellence, but, great as were the supreme artists of the past individually, there is, he argues, no point in emulating them, in doing again what they have done. What one can do is to possess the whole, to *be* the man for which all art exists, the perfect recipient:

> I have not chanted verse like Homer, no—
> Nor swept string like Terpander, no—nor carved
> And painted men like Phidias and his friend:
> I am not great as they are, point by point.
> But I have entered into sympathy
> With these four, running these into one soul,
> Who, separate, ignored each others' arts.
> Say, is it nothing that I know them all?

He is a man of superb Apollonian accomplishment; he is more than a temporal king, since his mind surveys and possesses all things, rather like Tennyson's poet in *The Palace of Art*. Besides, his own practice in the various arts has attained considerable success. If there is any supreme purpose or meaning in art, he ought, certainly, to be a high type of being, one who has built *all* the arts into himself and so reached 'the very crown and proper end of life'. And yet, what of death? The King to whom Cleon is writing will have nothing better than a 'brazen statue' to commemorate him. And can the artist claim more? What has art to say to death? These constant references to sculpture underline the far-reaching implications of the statue-coming-to-life in *The Winter's Tale*: 'What fine chisel could ever yet cut breath?' (V. iii. 78).

Cleon feels himself utterly ineffectual. He has imitated life, understood life, but not lived it; and even if his works persist, that gives him as a man no immortality. Art is not *being*:

> Because in my great epos I display
> How divers men young, strong, fair, wise, can act—
> Is this as though I acted? if I paint,
> Carve the young Phoebus, am I therefore young?

Though growing old, yet every day his 'sense of joy' becomes 'more acute'; his soul is 'intensified by power and insight', 'more enlarged' and 'keen'; and yet he is failing in body. Has God no more to offer? No word from above regarding *another stage* of being?

> I dare at times imagine to my need
> Some future state revealed to us by Zeus,
> Unlimited in capability
> For joy, as this is in desire for joy,
> —To seek which, the joy-hunger forces us:
> That, stung by straitness of our life, made strait
> On purpose to make prized the life at large—
> Freed by the throbbing impulse we call death,
> We burst there as the worm into the fly,
> Who, while a worm still, wants his wings. But no!
> Zeus has not yet revealed it; and, alas,
> He must have done so, were it possible!

Cleon concludes his epistle by replying to a request by Protus that he should forward a letter to one 'Paulus'. Cleon admits having heard of him and his preaching concerning 'Christus'. But surely no wisdom can be expected from a 'barbarian Jew'. He has heard accounts of Paulus' followers:

> And (as I gathered from a bystander)
> Their doctrine could be held by no sane man.

The ironic conclusion is exquisite, and pregnant.

We must notice: (i) the valuable thought of *all* the arts, with their corresponding senses and perceptions, together accomplishing what none alone or in separation could do; (ii) the implied inadequacy of artistic enjoyment or practice to meet the human problem; (iii) the demand of the soul to live beyond old-age; and (iv) the impinging of Christianity on the ineffectuality of Hellenic paganism, coming as, in Nietzsche's terms, an influx of the Dionysian on an effete Apollonian culture. We may remember

Arnold's attribution of action to Hebraism and thought to Hellenism, in *Culture and Anarchy*. We may suppose that the real incarnation of art in its totality would indeed give us a superman; would somehow correspond to the resurrection from the statue in *The Winter's Tale*. We should note, too, that what we hear through trance-mediumship of conditions on higher planes beyond death suggests that we shall there enjoy a totality of sense-perception unlimited to the body's separate inlets, which are at death broken to make possible a greater, sense-summing, experience; no longer, as Marvell has it in his *Dialogue between the Soul and the Body*, 'blinded with an eye' and 'deaf with the drumming of an ear'. But intimations of any such richer stages of being can only mature from a deeper, more Hebraic or Dionysian, experience than Cleon has achieved. With Nietzsche the Dionysian, conceived as the *alpha* and *omega* of creation, is equated with music; and it is significant that the only art that Browning unconditionally honours as the voice of the eternal, the resolver of antinomies and healer of mortality, is the music of *Abt Vogler*; and even so, it seems that one must live, be identified with, the music, both compose and perform it *ex tempore*; not merely listen, or write it down. One must *be* the music. Let us turn to this central poem.

There is a recurring poetic association of music with sacred or numinous architectures. On its most obvious level we have Milton's *Il Penseroso*:

> But let my due feet never fail
> To walk the studious cloister's pale,
> And love the high embowed roof,
> With antique pillars massy proof,
> And storied windows richly dight,
> Casting a dim religious light.
> There let the pealing organ blow
> To the full voic'd choir below,
> In service high and anthems clear,
> As may with sweetness, through mine ear,
> Dissolve me into ecstasies,
> And bring all Heaven before mine eyes.

That is simple enough. But more often the music is the creative, Dionysian, source, aspiring to structure, and therefore, at the limit, as we find in Eliot's *Burnt Norton* (V), to stillness, or silence. We may recall the palace built by organ music in *Paradise Lost* (I, 705–32); the music-built palace of *Lamia*; and the dome which the poet wishes to build 'in air' by the aid of 'music loud and long' recaptured from the Abyssinian maid's song-symphony, in *Kubla Khan*. We may assert a poetic equivalence, pretty nearly, between sacred, or otherwise mystical, or numinous, architectures and music; both distend intellect beyond its capacities, or to their limit, as in Byron's stanzas on St. Peter's, 'all musical in its immensities' (*Childe Harold*, IV. 156). Byron was fascinated by Goethe's description of architecture as 'frozen music' (Journal, 17 Nov. 1813; LJ, II. 326).

So much may be said in introduction to Browning's *Abt Vogler*, wherein for once an art is allowed by the poet to measure up to and indeed outdistance those eternally valid and indomitable energies that to him are the inmost stuff of human nature.

Abt Vogler is an organist who describes his art as a palace-building art recalling the magic powers of Solomon to enlist both 'angels' *and* 'demons' to 'pile him a palace straight' for his loved one. So, too, is his own 'beautiful building' made of music:

Would it might tarry like his, the beautiful building of mine,
This which my keys in a crowd pressed and importuned to raise!
Ah, one and all, how they helped, would dispart now and now combine,
Zealous to hasten the work, heighten their master his praise!
And one would bury his brow with a blind plunge down to hell,
Burrow a while and build, broad on the roots of things,
Then up again swim into sight, having based me my palace well,
Founded it, fearless of flame, flat on the nether springs.

And another would mount and march, like the excellent minion he was,
Ay, another and yet another, one crowd but with many a crest,
Raising my rampired walls of gold as transparent as glass,

> Eager to do and die, yield each his place to the rest:
> For higher still and higher (as a runner tips with fire,
>   When a great illumination surprises a festal night—
> Outlining round and round Rome's dome from space to spire)
>   Up, the pinnacled glory reached, and the pride of my soul was in
>   sight.

The conception makes of music a concrete reality that directly
meets Rudolf Steiner's theory of sound as carving out etheric
solids. We are, in so far as we take the metaphor seriously—and
all good metaphors should be taken seriously—beyond all rational
categories, and plunged into possibilities outspacing normal
perceptions. Music is regarded, as it was by Schopenhauer and
Nietzsche, as the creative origin. It is here more than an art; it is
a living act of the soul, since Abt Vogler is not merely composing,
but simultaneously performing, and therefore in a unique sense
living, the music. The transcendence is realized 'all through music
and me'; the inmost 'I' of the creator is, as with Pope's Pindar in
The Temple of Fame, who is shown as *melting* into his music,
engaged; there is an identification, corresponding to Eliot's 'you
are the music, while the music lasts' (*The Dry Salvages*, V).

As for painting, it is, says Abt Vogler, static, a thing, as Nietzsche tells us, of calm Apollonian contemplation merely; it just
stands—though logic would demand that Abt Vogler should
sound also into the painter's experience in composition, which may
have been as vivid as his own—to be looked at. All he observes
is that its 'process', presumably when completed, is not so 'wonder-
worth'; not, that is, part of the wonder. As for poetry, where
there certainly *is* a process, yet you can apply reason to it and
understand its laws. Music is beyond all that:

> But here is the finger of God, a flash of the will that can,
>   Existent behind all laws . . .

'The will' is here used as Nietzsche and Schopenhauer use it to
denote the central divine, or cosmic, purpose. Even though the
palace *seems* to dissolve, the faith is next transferred to God as the
source and therefore presumably the ratifier of the experience.
The music-palace has revealed, or created, the eternal stuff which

somehow knows no transience and assures us that 'there shall never be one lost good'. What is incomplete here, is with God completed:

On the earth the broken arcs; in the heaven, a perfect round.

Every fine longing is there established, 'not its semblance, but itself', eternity affirming 'the conception of an hour'. Especially, all the failings, the impossibilities, the *thwarted* things, the tragedies of life, are 'music sent up to God'; so:

Enough that he heard it once; we shall hear it by and by.

Failure is earnest of triumph; the paradox within all tragedy is, as with Nietzsche, resolved in terms of music:

The rest may reason and welcome: 'tis we musicians know.[1]

The eternity-symbols of *Abt Vogler* should be compared with the remarkable passage in *An Epistle containing the strange medical experience of Karshish, the Arab physician*, wherein the raised Lazarus is imagined, after the experience of the richer existence beyond death, as suffering from his forced return to the 'thread' of earthly life, of time,

Which runs across some vast distracting orb
Of glory on either side that meagre thread,
Which, conscious of, he must not enter yet . . .

All normal valuations, based as they are on considerations of time, are now to Lazarus meaningless. To him 'right and wrong' exist 'across, and not along', that is, at right angles to, 'this black thread through the blaze'. Such intuitions form the living core of Browning's work.

In discussion of these clustering symbolisms we are near the heart of poetry. Alone of the arts poetry sums all the rest; in it sound and image, thought and sight, are fused. Rhythm and music project it, with all its weighty substances, into activity,

---

[1] Beside the views of music expressed by Nietzsche and Browning, we may set a passage from *The Testament of Beauty* (II. 825-39), where it is observed that animals can respond to music, but not to pictures, or to their own reflections. The visual arts depend on mental development.

according to the scheme defined in Nietzsche's *Birth of Tragedy*. We may feel, at choice moments, that all human and other creations are as architecture musically, and so spiritually, based, as in that gem of Tennyson's *Tithonus*:

> Like that strange song I heard Apollo sing,
> While Ilion like a mist rose into towers.

It is not surprising that a minor poet such as Arthur O'Shaughnessy should, in handling such symbols, have been raised above his normal level. He is writing, or singing, of poets:

> We are the music-makers,
>   And we are the dreamers of dreams,
> Wandering by lone sea-breakers,
>   And sitting by desolate streams;—
> World-losers and world-forsakers,
>   On whom the pale moon gleams:
> Yet we are the movers and shakers
>   Of the world for ever, it seems.
>
> With wonderful deathless ditties
> We build up the world's great cities,
>   And out of a fabulous story
>   We fashion an empire's glory:
> One man with a dream, at pleasure,
>   Shall go forth and conquer a crown;
> And three with a new song's measure
>   Can trample a kingdom down.
>
> We, in the ages lying
>   In the buried past of the earth,
> Built Nineveh with our sighing,
>   And Babel itself in our mirth;
> And o'erthrew them with prophesying
>   To the old of the new world's worth;
> For each age is a dream that is dying,
>   Or one that is coming to birth.

How true those last few lines are of our popular song-cults, today. The poem's expanded version, which continues with a number of less weighted stanzas, is weaker. There appears to be both

danger and safety in these basic symbolisms: it is when O'Shaughnessy leaves them that authenticity sags.

We may watch something not dissimilar happening with his
more famous compatriot, W. B. Yeats, whose two outstanding
poems, *Sailing to Byzantium* and *Byzantium*, are both compacted,
as his other work is not, of symbolisms forcing on us the opposition of art and nature, the static and the dynamic, in significant
interplay. Both poems are rich and colourful creations. 'Byzantium' brings all its famous historic and sacred associations to act
on us as did Samarkand in Flecker's *Hassan*; or, rather differently,
Kubla Khan in Coleridge's poem. In each a sharply located
historic magnificence lends definition and detonation to a poetic
universal. Byzantium and Samarkand are the more poetically
valuable in that as sacred cities both, and Byzantium especially,
suggest a blend of the secular and the sacred.

Sailing to Byzantium presents its terms in stark opposition. The
poet, like Browning's Cleon, is growing old, and like him he
endures a painful discrepancy between ageing body and lively
soul. Like Browning's Rabbi ben Ezra, he demands that the soul
should rejoice as the body wanes, and accordingly plants his hopes
in 'monuments of unageing intellect', monuments of its (i.e. the
soul's) 'own magnificence'; that is, works of art, intellectually and,
if only by metaphor, plastically conceived. So he prays to the

> . . . sages standing in God's holy fire
> As in the gold mosaic of a wall

to be his masters and rescue him from the natural order; from
the young 'in one another's arms', the 'dying generations' of
birds, and the teeming fishes of river and sea, 'fish, flesh or fowl',
'whatever is begotten, born and dies'. The 'sensual music' of
physical life—music, by an interesting transposition, here accom-
panying the biological—is set in contrast to a metallic symbolism:

> Once out of nature I shall never take
> My bodily form from any natural thing,
> But such a form as Grecian goldsmiths make
> Of hammered gold and gold enamelling
> To keep a drowsy emperor awake;

> Or set upon a golden bough to sing
> To lords and ladies of Byzantium
> Of what is past, or passing, or to come.

The metal bird both corresponds to the soul-body, in some eastern cults called the 'diamond' body, of the spirit after death, and symbolizes an all-seeing eternity. The bird itself is a sheer artefact, but then Byzantium is here chosen to symbolize the soul's refuge precisely because of the metallic, stiff, other-worldly, yet rich, qualities of its especially sacred art: 'gold mosaic' is a typifying phrase. In contrast, we have summer, 'all summer long', sensuality and almost violent biological fecundity. The opposition is stark. The heart, 'fastened to a dying animal', and yet, like Cleon, 'sick with desire', can only cry to be gathered 'into the artifice of eternity'. 'Artifice' is a deliberately cold word, set against the insult of 'animal'.

The second, and more complex, poem, *Byzantium*, presents a similar contrast, though with a more satisfying fusion. We are in the Emperor's palace. The 'unpurged images of day' give place to night's purer images; the 'drunken soldiery', now 'abed', establish a contrast of riotous life and sequent quietude. We pass through the singing of 'night-walkers' and the numinous summons of the 'great cathedral gong' to

> A starlit or a moonlit dome disdains
> All that man is,
> All mere complexities,
> The fury and the mire of human veins.

Through night and eternity-symbols we pass next to intuition of an 'image', human yet a 'shade'; more 'shade' (that is, spiritual) than 'man', and yet fully concrete and so 'more image than a shade'. We are in the world of death, unwinding 'the mummy, cloth' which is also the unwinding of the 'winding' maze-path into 'Hades'.[1]

---

[1] The ancient symbol of the 'maze' or 'labyrinth' used with respect to the passage from this life to the next is discussed throughout my brother's *Cumaean Gates*, reissued in *Vergil: Epic and Anthropology*, 1967; see Index II. For the 'Golden Bough', which occurs in both Byzantium poems, a as passport to the other world, see p. 158 and Index II.

This being's 'mouth', having neither 'moisture' nor 'breath', can 'summon' the 'breathless mouths' of the dead to itself. The poet is aware of some more than human, but not inhuman, presence:

> I hail the superhuman;
> I call it death-in-life and life-in-death.

The poem has moved from an earthly emperor's palace by night to a sense of a life in, or beyond, death.

We are again introduced to a golden bird, now felt as neither 'bird' nor 'handiwork', but as a 'miracle'; on a 'star-lit golden bough', compared to the 'cocks of Hades', and angry at the moon with its changes, and reminders perhaps of the sun, preferring its own supernal nature; in its 'glory of changeless metal' spurning the lower nature and 'all complexities of mire or blood'. It seems more *alive* than before. Again, we return to the Emperor's hall, now a place beyond nature where 'flit' flames independent of the natural order, 'flames begotten of flame'; and to them come the 'blood-begotten spirits', the phrase underlining what might seem the paradox of the natural, biological, order as the begetting source of a spiritual after-life. There is a death-agony, but it is a move beyond 'complexities' and 'fury'; at once a 'dying into a dance', and a dying into 'an agony of trance', an entry into a supernatural but unhurting flame which cannot 'singe'.

Our conclusion asserts a victory. Multitudinous spirits are seen riding on 'the dolphin's mire and blood', that is, man riding his own physical life in violent motion. Next the Emperor's 'golden smithies' are said to 'break the flood', annihilate the sensual and biological, and all violent action in time, while 'marbles of the dancing-floor'—a neat fusion of solidity and harmonious motion—vanquish the 'bitter furies of complexity'.

We have the gong, sacred architecture, rich metals, marble, and flames, all balanced against 'the fury and the mire of human veins', violent motion, the 'dolphin' (animal of watery and so passional—as Colin Still called it—life), and 'the flood'. The poem ends with the breaking of

Those images that yet
Fresh images beget,
That dolphin-torn, that gong-tormented sea.

'Dolphin-torn' suggests the violent motion of things in the order
of time, nature and passion; the 'gong-tormented sea' is the
biological order ruthlessly dominated by the transcendent. But
what are the 'images'? Earlier, 'image' was used for a form
between 'man' and 'shade'; spirit 'flames' were 'begotton of flame',
not of other, plural, flames; and the spirit of man was, strangely,
'blood-begotten'. Our conclusion seems to blend the two sorts of
begetting, answering the earlier paradox by adumbration of the
truth that spirit has been functioning from the start, its 'image',
perhaps with a reference to God making men in His own 'image' in
Genesis, first at work in ceaseless human propagation and then
making man, as spirit, ride his 'dolphin', or physical body,
through a nature both 'torn' by man's own violent course and
'tormented' by the gong summoning from the flames and gold.

The fusion here is more satisfying than in *Sailing to Byzantium*;
the impressions of the 'superhuman', of 'miracle', of living spirit-
flames, and above all of the 'dance', together with the sense we
get of assured, purposeful, and living activity on the part of the
more metallic and supernal entities, leaves us with a resultant
harmony. The two poems most admirably serve to define our
main opposites, in contrast and creative interplay. They, and
especially the second, provide fascinating exemplars of the way
great poetry chooses to base its more visionary structures on a
tangible foundation. Logic is discounted. We move from
historic Byzantium through night and sleep to a transformation
whereby the Emperor has suddenly become God and his palace
paradise; much the same happened in Coleridge's *Kubla Khan*.
The *Byzantium* poems will surely be more and more clearly
recognized as Yeats' greatest work; they stand out proudly from
his more personal records and more ascetic manner; and their
outstanding importance derives from the nature of the symbols
used, enlisting all our resources of known reality and sense-
perception to make us enjoy a more than sensory recognition.

VII

George Sturt and the English Humanitarian Tradition

E. D. MACKERNESS

IN a letter written to Mrs. Charles West on 4 April 1924, George Sturt complained bitterly about his failure to obtain much substantial recognition from the 'literary pundits' of the day. He went on to bemoan the fact that '"George Bourne" now known as George Sturt, is never mentioned; I suspect he is looked upon as an intelligent artisan: he is not fashionable . . .' When Sturt wrote those words, he was in considerable physical and mental distress; repeated cardiac disorders had almost completely paralysed him, and coherent speech was virtually impossible. His handwriting was reduced to a mere scrawl; and though he was to live for another three years, he realized that he could not hope to publish much more. His last effort at extended composition— *A Small Boy in the Sixties* (1927)—was not in fact produced until after his death. Yet Sturt's agonized self-pity, though understandable in the circumstances, was not altogether justified. His recent book, *The Wheelwright's Shop* (1923), was warmly received; though hardly calculated to establish Sturt as a 'fashionable' writer, it did at least induce a *Times Literary Supplement* reviewer to observe (31 May 1923) that 'It shows in the author a combination of the gifts of the handicraftsman, the actual maker of things, with the powers of a writer, in a way not common in English literature . . .' The reputation which Sturt had created for himself under the pseudonym of 'George Bourne' was sustained for many years. By 1913 both the early *Bettesworth Book* (1901) and its sequel *Memoirs of a Surrey Labourer* (1907) had found their way into Duckworth's 'Readers' Library': in 1920 a reprint of *Change in the Village* (1912) appeared: and on 11 November 1922 Jonathan

Cape himself visited Sturt at Vine Cottage, Farnham, in order to present him with an advance copy of the illustrated first edition of *A Farmer's Life*. So on the whole, it cannot be claimed that Sturt's literary achievement was entirely ignored by the critics. Indeed, the 'pundits'—if we include among them reviewers for *The Observer*, *The Nation* and *The Manchester Guardian*—treated him generously. A new edition of *Change in the Village* was issued as recently as 1955, and *The Wheelwright's Shop* is now available in paperback form. Yet in spite of the classic status which these two books enjoy, there has been a tendency in some quarters to look upon Sturt with suspicion because of his apparent idealization of an earlier period. For this reason it may be useful to examine his fundamental allegiances in order to establish whether it is quite fair to dismiss him as merely an uncritical *laudator temporis acti*. In this essay I shall argue that quite apart from his distinction as an authority on craftsmanship and the 'dynamics' of cultural transition, Sturt takes his place within a specifically English tradition of sentiment which links his name with those of several other figures who are usually held in greater reverence than he is.

I

George Sturt's literary career began quite modestly in the 1880's, when he contributed a number of topical essays to *The Commonweal*, the journal of the Socialist League. By this time Sturt had settled down as manager of the family wheelwright business in East Street, Farnham—a career he did not relish, but which he felt it was his duty to make something of. Although distracted by day-to-day chores, Sturt was unable to repress the *cacoethes scribendi* which drove him to attempt several forms of literary composition. Over a long period in the 1890's he worked hard on a novel, which was eventually published under the title of *A Year's Exile* in 1898; but Sturt also felt a strong disposition to produce non-fiction and would have given much to be able to shape the somewhat raw philosophizings which appear in the earlier parts of his *Journals* (commenced in October 1890) into acceptable essays on political and sociological problems. In *The Wheelwright's Shop* he tells us of his fondness for Carlyle, Ruskin and Emerson; and his *Commonweal* papers (on such subjects as sweated labour, the Dock Strike of 1889, and Ruskin's industrial enterprises) suggest that during his twenties Sturt was assimilating 'progressive' doctrines with avidity. Some form of 'Socialism' seemed to him the only means of eradicating 'this slavery to necessity (embracing say three fourths of our population) . . .' of which he wrote in his *Journals* for 24 November 1890. But Sturt's Socialism, like H. G. Wells's, was 'pre-Marxian' in the sense that it was derived from popular propagandists rather than from formal exponents of political theory. Sturt had nothing, however, of Wells's flair for analysis and cogent formulation: he could not envisage new social organizations with the boldness which characterizes such works as *Anticipations* (1902) or *Socialism and the Family* (1906). From time to time Sturt was to castigate Wells for the latter's indifference to the principle of organic growth: he distrusted policies which were, as he thought, based on a passion 'for machinery, for organization . . .' (*Journals*, 1 March 1916). Sturt maintained that in their zeal to reconstitute society the Fabians (and those who sympathized with them) undervalued human spontaneity: he had little hesitation in placing George Bernard Shaw among the bright superior people whose confidence in purely intellectual solutions to the problems of the day betrayed a certain disregard of traditional sanctions. Yet there was one leading Socialist—H. S. Salt (1851–1939)—for whom Sturt did profess a sincere admiration. It is impossible to discover whether the esteem was mutual; but there can be no doubt that Sturt found Salt's counsels congenial and derived from him a form of enlightenment which, for a time at any rate, was extremely acceptable.

For some years, Salt and his wife, Kate Joynes, lived in a cottage at Tilford, a short distance from Farnham. Sturt was in touch with Salt at this time and may well have read the article, 'A Sunday on the Surrey Hills' (*Pall Mall Gazette*, 28 April 1888) in which Shaw described a visit to the Salts and incidentally poured scorn on the joys of rural residence. According to Shaw, Salt was 'a man of exceptional intelligence on most subjects'; a brilliant classical scholar, he had resigned his post as a master at

H

Eton in tacit protest against the social injustices condoned by those
who regarded wealth and privilege as part of the natural order of
things. It was, of course, unheard of for a man in Salt's position
to profess sympathy with 'Socialism': but Salt, like his brother-
in-law James Joynes, was fiercely determined in his convictions.
He had been profoundly influenced by the writings of another
Etonian, Shelley, and in his numerous books and pamphlets he
attacked certain aspects of later Victorian society with a Shelleyan
fervour. Sturt particularly admired Salt's detailed *Life of Henry
David Thoreau* (1890), a work which came as a revelation and
made Sturt conscious that there was a great affinity between himself and the author of *Walden*. Salt also published studies of
James Thomson ('B.V.') and Richard Jefferies; but he is better
known for his work on Godwin, Hogg and Shelley. One can
gather the importance of Shelley in Salt's view of things by
comparing his *Shelley's Principles* . . . (1892) with *Tennyson as a
Thinker* (1893), a work which shows how heartily Salt joined in
what A. C. Bradley in 1929 called 'The Reaction against Tennyson'. 'Every great artist,' Salt affirms,

> must sympathize with humanity, but it is not necessary that he
> should engage in theological or social disputation. Art divorced
> from ethical principles is bad enough; but art in conjunction
> with an intolerant and wrong-headed view of ethical principles
> may perhaps be still worse.[1]

The implications of this so far as Tennyson is concerned need
not be enlarged upon. In Salt's estimation, Shelley was pre-
eminently the right kind of poet and Tennyson was not. But
the idolization of Shelley in the last quarter of the nineteenth
century was one of those things which helped to foster the climate
of opinion in which non-violent revolutionaries such as George
Sturt could get their bearings.

Shelley's ethical idealism was also relevant to the great movement in which H. S. Salt was a leading figure for many years—
Humanitarianism. There are traces of the Humanitarian spirit
in writers who lived long before Shelley; but Salt held that it

---

[1] *Tennyson as a Thinker*, p. 10.

reached its highest point of philosophical development in the works of Arthur Schopenhauer, and certainly there is a cogent exposition of it in Schopenhauer's *World as Will and Idea* (1819), of which an authoritative English translation appeared in 1883. In its nineteenth-century guise, Humanitarianism may be described as a creed which had as its object the promotion of social sympathy in the widest sense, together with a serious concern for a proper relationship between man and the rest of animated creation. Its ramifications were enormous; it insisted on the exposure of commonly tolerated abuses, and advocated the achievement of radical reforms in spheres untouched by orthodox legislation. Humanitarianism made an especial appeal to those who felt that with the advent of the twentieth century a new social order was bound to come into being. 'The present age,' Salt wrote,

> is confessedly one of transition, in religious and moral belief; the old faiths are dying or dead, and we look for some new motive-power to take their place in the future. This coming creed, which shall interpret and reconcile the Babel of conflicting utterances by which we are now bewildered, seems likely to be none other than a religion of humanity ... [leading to] a society in which all harmless and healthy life shall be free to develop itself unrestricted and uninjured ...[1]

Remarks comparable to these are frequent in George Sturt's early *Journals*, as for instance in the entry for 24 November 1890 where he envisages that under some form of Socialism 'the yearning undeveloped aims even of grown and sophisticated men would suddenly spring to life ...' Sturt did not propose to invoke a 'religion of humanity' as such; but he did look forward to the evolution of a more comprehensive form of democracy than any the politicians had so far conceived—this being the subject of his unfinished and unpublished book, *Democratic Faith*, which was abandoned soon after the First World War broke out.

Yet in spite of his respect for Salt, George Sturt was unable to identify himself completely with the Humanitarians, largely because their thinking depended on the adoption of absolutist

[1] *Humanitarianism* ... (1896), p. 26.

positions. On the subject of vegetarianism, for instance (which most Humanitarians advocated), it is impossible to be entirely consistent. Sturt loathed cruelty to animals just as much as Salt did; but he recognized that—as Arthur Schopenhauer points out —not all members of the animal kingdom can be treated with equal deference. This point is hinted at in a letter from Thomas Hardy to the Secretary of the Humanitarian League;[1] and Sturt, influenced as Hardy was by the implications of Darwinism, must have felt that in many respects the Humanitarians were not quite looking nature 'in the face', so to speak. While agreeing that the infliction of suffering in the name of 'sport' was a despicable business, Sturt felt that there was something ludicrous in trying to 'humanize' a cat by restraining it from catching mice. Sturt would not have agreed with George Moore when in *Confessions of a Young Man* (1886) he wrote that 'Humanitarianism is a pigsty, where liars, hypocrites, and the obscene in spirit congregate; it has been so since the great Jew conceived it, and it will be so till the end . . .':[2] yet in *Lucy Bettesworth* (1913) Sturt argued that 'the tender anthropomorphism of delicately nurtured people'[3] might easily be taken too far. The peasantry whose daily lives he described in *Change in the Village* could not afford false delicacy; their hard struggle for survival forbade the kind of squeamishness which Jude Fawley experienced when called upon to slaughter a pig at Marygreen.[4] In more general terms, however, Sturt felt obliged to dissociate himself from men like Salt because he could see that excessive enthusiasm for reform is likely to warp an otherwise normal personality. It is indeed an odd paradox that cultivated warm-heartedness often leads to egregious behaviour: and those who are most anxious to ameliorate the lives of others fall short in the cultivation of their own general sensibility. Not all forms of meliorism are equally admirable; and Sturt deprecated any proposals for the betterment of the lower classes 'which might impair their innate toughness of fibre'.

[1] 10 April 1910. See F. E. Hardy, *The Life of Thomas Hardy 1840–1928* (1962), p. 349.

[2] *Confessions of a Young Man* (Heinemann, 'Travellers' Library', 1928), p. 217.

[3] *Lucy Bettesworth*, p. 83.

[4] Hardy, *Jude the Obscure* (1895), Part First, Chapter X.

II

Sturt's views on many political and moral issues reveal a certain amount of obduracy and confusion. Yet it is clear that in spite of his admiration for H. S. Salt, Edward Carpenter and other 'cranks', he cannot be looked upon as a Humanitarian in the sense of the word made current by them. On 27 March 1895 Salt had sent Sturt a copy of the new journal, *Humanity*: it took Sturt two hours to explain in a letter to Salt why he felt unable to number himself among the humanitarians. Yet there is another sense in which this term may be applied to him. In his *Journals* for 18 October 1914 he spoke of the possibility of a true 'democratic faith' eventually emerging through the smoke and stir of present social upheavals, and stressed the value for English people of what he called 'the Wordsworthian or humanitarian attitude'. This attitude had many social implications: it was 'a part of England's spontaneous living—a part of folk-life . . .' And for Sturt it lent a special significance to English literature: 'I would use the famous writers,' he wrote, 'chiefly as doorways into England's inner life . . .' (*Journals*, 30 May 1917). We may have reservations about this particular *use* of our poetry and prose; but implicit in Sturt's way of putting things is a view of 'humanity' which he was merely carrying over from writers of earlier generations.

After leaving Farnham Grammar School in 1884 George Sturt received no further formal education; but he was a reasonably well-read man, with a considerable knowledge of modern literature. Apart from fiction, he was particularly impressed by the work of aestheticians, historians and social critics. 'Ah, if you would only read Tom Paine in the proper spirit . . .' exclaims Peter Shirley at the end of Act II of Shaw's *Major Barbara*. Sturt *had* read Carlyle, Ruskin, Emerson, Whitman and Thoreau in the right spirit. Although he found Carlyle's power-worship distasteful, he applauded the energy with which the author of *Sartor Resartus* was able to proclaim that 'the English Radical may become the English rebuilder' (see *Journals*, 22 August 1892); Ruskin's work persuaded him that 'dignity of labour' was not merely a cliché. The 'authentic vitality' of *Leaves of Grass* was comparable in its way with Pater's 'new hedonism': Thoreau showed that it was possible for men to live on a plane of existence outside the reach of mundane trivialities. For some time the 'philosophy' set out in Thoreau's major writings seemed to fill Sturt's mind with a necessary stimulus; later on he found a similar enjoyment in the Pater of *Imaginary Portraits*. But when he himself began to publish he gradually revealed in his successive books a certain kinship with a number of English authors who belonged to 'an earlier period in which England and Englishmen were harder, simpler, less sophisticated, than today ...'[1] The authors concerned include Gilbert White, Thomas Bewick, John Constable and Wordsworth. If an apology is needed for incorporating Constable in this group, it must be that the artist's letters and lecture notes disclose a literary sensibility of some power.[2] But collectively these names represent a distinctive mode of responsiveness—continued in later writers such as George Eliot and Hardy—which is compatible with most of Sturt's published work. To this 'tradition' he owed an allegiance greater than he was able to summon up when trying to assimilate his own brand of Socialism to that with which *fin-de-siècle* Humanitarianism was in alliance.

The *Natural History of Selborne* (1789) was one of Sturt's favourite books. In an essay on 'Our Primitive Knowledge' he remarked on Gilbert White's 'truly marvellous' habit of recording details of the rural scene.[3] The Curate of Selborne may not have had much practical skill in farming; yet his knowledge of agricultural processes was wide, and he had a gift for rendering in vivid idiomatic prose much local lore which he had derived direct from the tenants of the land he owned.[4] White was fortunate in being, like Sturt after him, a 'provincial': this enabled him to become acquainted with the particularities of rustic economy in all its aspects. 'To know the neighbourhood through and through,'

---

[1] *Lucy Bettesworth*, p. 244.

[2] An abstract of a lecture delivered by Constable in 1833 is given in Chapter XVIII of C. R. Leslie's *Life*.

[3] 'Our Primitive Knowledge' is Chapter XIII of *Lucy Bettesworth*.

[4] See in this connection Chapter VI ('Genuine Countryman') of Cecil S. Emden, *Gilbert White in his Village* (1956).

Sturt wrote in 1919, 'this (is) the way to live...';[1] and in many ways Gilbert White's existence can be said to have been full and gratifying. 'Thus to learn their country, field by field, has been one among the many studies of the English for fourteen hundred years . . .' Sturt tells us in 'Our Primitive Knowledge':[2] and he goes on to contrast the kind of knowledge envisaged here with the substitute for it offered by agricultural colleges. In his *Journals*, Sturt occasionally tried to emulate Gilbert White's descriptions of bird and animal behaviour. But the style of *The Natural History of Selborne* is inimitable, and it would be a mistake to regard Sturt as a latter-day Gilbert White. He knew very little of the scientific literature—Aristotle, Linnaeus, John Ray—on which White continually drew, and as a field naturalist the earlier author was incomparably superior. Yet the two men took great pains to register the effect of environment on human life and aspirations. But whereas Gilbert White's notes on village industries—as, for instance, in Letter V of *Selborne*—are mostly plain documentary ('. . . Besides the employment from husbandry, the men work in hop gardens, of which we have many; and fell and bark timber. In the spring and summer the women weed the corn . . .', etc.) Sturt's rendering of similar material conveys a sense of arduousness and monotony in day-to-day labours which finds no parallel in the writings of Gilbert White. In *Change in the Village*, for example, he writes:

> It may be added that many of the women . . . were field-workers. . . . Far beyond the valley they had to go to earn money at hop-tying, haymaking, harvesting, potato-picking, swede-trimming, and at such work they came immediately, just as the men did, under conditions which made it a vice to flinch . . .[3]

The preoccupations which underlie such passages as this serve to remind us that many significant features of English social history—the 'Swing' riots, Chartism and the formation of the National Agricultural Union—stand between Gilbert White and

[1] Preface to *William Smith Potter and Farmer*.
[2] *Lucy Bettesworth*, pp. 213–4.
[3] *Change in the Village* (ed. of 1955), p. 23.

the author of *The Bettesworth Book*. The two men felt, however, a conscientious disposition to support—in deference to the real interests of their neighbours—the principle of conservation rather than innovation. So we find Gilbert White opposing schemes for enclosing parts of Selborne[1] and George Sturt insisting in *Change in the Village* that the enclosure of the common was responsible more than anything else for rendering village life so void of hope and interest.[2]

The personality of Thomas Bewick (1753–1828) as revealed in his *Memoir* (1862) was one of singular sweetness and sagacity. He was primarily a master craftsman and not an 'intellectual'; but in his own way he was dedicated to the task of revealing the wonders of God in the works of Creation: James Thomson was his favourite poet. Unlike George Sturt, Bewick was a Christian who maintained that 'the highest character a man can hope to attain to in this life is that of being a religious philosopher . . .'[3] The reason for linking his name with that of Sturt is that in a period notable for coarseness of manners and the identification of 'manliness' with brute strength, Bewick showed a pronounced sense of compassion for innocent creatures. It was one of Sturt's beliefs—some would regard it as an illusion—that what differentiated the modern period from earlier times was the present-day reluctance to resort *habitually* to acts of cruelty and violence when dealing with other sentient beings. In his *Memoir*, Bewick tells how he passed through an early phase in which he delighted in hunting and capturing wild life; but after a time such pursuits ceased to satisfy him. On one occasion he had thrown a missile into a tree and brought down a bullfinch. 'It was alive,' he tells us,

> and looked me piteously in the face: and, as I thought, could it have spoken, it would have asked me why I had taken away its life. I felt greatly hurt at what I had done . . . I turned it over and over, admiring its plumage, its feet, its bill, and every part of it. . . . This was the last bird I killed . . .[4]

[1] See R. Holt-White, *Life and Letters of Gilbert White* (1901), II. 260–1.
[2] See *Change in the Village*, ed. cit., p. 86–7.
[3] *A Memoir of Thomas Bewick, Written by Himself* . . . (1862), p. 278.
[4] Ibid., p. 21–2.

It is unlikely that Sturt knew this passage; but there is a remarkable parallel to it in his *Journals* for 14 December 1890. On that day Sturt had been out walking with his brother Frank and had noticed the thrushes feeding on holly berries. Then he thought he heard a gun shot, and reflected that it seemed particularly mean to be taking advantage of the birds in such bitterly cold weather. 'Nor can I see,' he goes on, 'that this brutality of "sport" holds in it any seeds of humanity, to grow up and choke it. It isn't every stone hits the bird aimed at, but not one fails to injure the thrower. . . .' The sentiment expressed here, though rather clumsily set out, is close to Bewick's; and from his *Memoir* we can see how Bewick came to be an agent, as it were—though Cowper and Blake might also be named in the same connection—in the great 'humanizing' movement which was in Sturt's mind when on 12 September 1926 he wrote that 'The discovery of delight in animal life—that discovery which is breaking down medieval cruelty—is one of the latest fruits of the spirituality of civilization'. A great number of creatures were, of course, killed for Bewick to use as subjects for his engravings, and curiously enough he approved of angling; but he shared with Sturt an abhorrence of the wanton pillaging of natural resources, as can be seen from his letter to Mr. Hopper on the regulation of the salmon fisheries and his denunciation of river pollution.[1] Bewick's republicanism and his concern for suffering humanity[2] recall Sturt's comments on 'Prussianism' and on the decline of 'folk' civilization made during the First World War (see, for example, his *Journals* for 11 and 18 October 1914). But perhaps the most interesting point of contact between the two individuals can be discerned when we read what Bewick has to say about the 'unspoiled, honourable, and kind people' he met when travelling among the highlands of Scotland.[3] Bewick's manner of observing the peasantry is very similar to Sturt's. He found the Highlanders a warm-hearted and generous race. 'Is it not to be regretted,' he asks,

---

[1] See Robert Robinson, *Thomas Bewick, his Life and Times* (1887), p. 151.

[2] Ibid., p. 76.

[3] *Memoir*, p. 89.

that agricultural improvements have taught the landlords, or chieftains, to turn numerous farms into one, and banish thousands of these hardy descendants of the ancient Britons . . . to seek asylum in foreign climes? In exchange for *men*, they have filled the country with sheep! Property, in every country, should be held sacred, but it should also have its bounds . . .[1]

Other parts of Bewick's work reveal an awareness—in places anticipating Sturt's—of the subtle ways in which economic necessity tends to impinge upon and impair the existing pattern of social relationships. This can be felt in all Bewick writes about the common people in the north of England: his descriptions of the 'bold peasantry' in Chapter III of the *Memoir* is strongly reminiscent of 'George Bourne' at his best.

Among English painters, George Sturt particularly admired the landscape artists such as David Cox, Alexander Nasmyth and John Constable. Like the latter, Sturt was fascinated by cloud formations and often described them in his *Journals*; but this is not the principal reason for mentioning the creator of 'The Hay Wain' in this essay. Constable was an individual of complex character; but after allowing for a certain impetuosity in his temperament, it is not difficult to discern that his type of sensibility—in particular his concern to preserve what in a letter to John Fisher he calls his 'natural dignity of mind'[2]—resembles George Sturt's in several particulars. Reverence for the diversity of nature, an instinctive ability to 'read' the significance of common objects, and a profound respect for the part played by *human* life in the world around him—these, as is well known, are the marks of Constable's genius. 'To his interest in natural history', writes R. B. Beckett,

Constable added a taste for antiquities. He loved any ancient buildings, from cottages to castles, which had grown to form part of the natural scenery around them; but their aesthetic charm was only part of their appeal. His imagination was

---

[1] *Memoir*, p. 90.
[2] The letter dates from 1821. See R. B. Beckett, *John Constable and the Fishers* . . . (1952), p. 66.

deeply moved by the story of the men who had built them and had lived in them . . .[1]

In *The Wheelwright's Shop* Sturt wrote about objects and attitudes which had survived from the time of 'Constables' England'— an England which antedated steam power and *laissez-faire* individualism. Constable was, of course, a more widely cultivated man than Sturt. But he would have appreciated the bearing of an essay such as Sturt's 'The Antiquarian Sentiment'.[2] This masterly piece of writing reveals the difference which exists between mere 'nostalgia' and an enlightened veneration for 'the continuity of life'. Once we demolish an old building, Sturt points out, not only does the fabric itself disappear, but much else is lost which cannot be supplied by a newer structure. 'The "much else",' he goes on,

> is the association with man's life, the intimation dimly vouchsafed to us of long succession of English folk. . . . Seldom thought of, perhaps, but almost always felt, this vision, or this sentiment rather, is called up only by things of venerable age. I have known it to be suggested, with sudden subtle touch upon the feelings, by the handle of an old rake or hoe cut long ago in a forgotten coppice, and worn to shining smoothness by hands that are now dead . . .[3]

A little later Sturt writes: 'The pity of it is that the busy world often ruins what it would fain keep, and admiring old things ignorantly, kills the life in them which alone makes them precious . . .'[4] It is the *life* in old things which Constable's canvases bring out so well: for him a barge or a watermill has much the same symbolic significance as a beck or a farm wagon had for Sturt—it presented (to borrow 'George Bourne's words in connection with local dialect) 'something genuinely English, something old yet young, something restful, lovable, and surely precious . . .'[5]

[1] *John Constable's Correspondence* V (ed. R. B. Beckett: Suffolk Records Society, 1967, Volume XI), p. 82.
[2] Section XVII of *Lucy Bettesworth*.
[3] Ibid., pp. 271-2.
[4] Ibid., p. 277.
[5] Ibid., p. 277.

Writing of a place in the neighbourhood of Farnham about to be 'opened up' by improved means of public transport, Sturt says that its chief beauty was 'more than is visible to eyesight. An intangible essence lingered there of an earlier, homelier England . . .'[1] But if Sturt *felt* this intangible essence, Constable had already suggested it in subtle gradations of colour. 'The Antiquarian Sentiment', indeed, might almost be looked upon as a commentary on the Suffolk artist's life-work. Sturt's own Constable-like serenity and inwardness is something which sets him apart from the avowedly 'country' writers who were numerous in the Edwardian and early Georgian periods.

It is with diffidence that the name of Wordsworth is brought into this discussion. For Sturt did not have a very close knowledge of Wordsworth's poetry. He once confessed (see *Journals*, 27 January 1900) that there was only one poem ('about the Woodland Girl') for which he really cared; and though he made some perceptive comments on *The Excursion* (*Journals*, 13 April 1913), he gives no evidence that he had thought much about those musings of the Wanderer (on conditions in factories) which would seem to be most relevant to his deepest interests.[2] There are, however, indications that in spite of this Sturt did appreciate what it is that Wordsworth gives us to rest on. Yet to discover the affinity between two men who were compounded of such different elements—and it is worth remarking that according to testimony brought to notice by H. D. Rawnsley, Wordsworth (unlike Sturt) stood aloof from the 'humble and rustic life' about which he knew so much[3]—we need to look not at Wordsworth's poetry but at his prose, and in particular the *Guide through the District of the Lakes in the North of England* . . . (originally published in 1810, but later expanded). This little book is stored with telling observations on lakeland scenery, and offers many harsh criticisms on the art of *creating* landscape; it also passes on to the discussion of social

---

[1] Ibid., p. 278.

[2] *The Excursion*, VIII. 82–230 and 252–333.

[3] See H. D. Rawnsley, 'Reminiscences of Wordsworth amongst the Peasantry of Westmoreland' in ed. William Knight, *Wordsworthiana. A Selection from papers read to the Wordsworth Society* (1889), pp. 81–119.

conditions in so far as they are affected by these phenomena. Wordsworth, like 'George Bourne' after him, deplores the agencies by which the 'inmates' of the Lake district were forced to set aside the long-established customs of living and the traditions of productive industry which made their daily toil rich and satisfying. He argues that so-called 'improvements' were gradually causing the small proprietors—whether 'estatesmen' or more substantial farmers—to give up the holdings which were their main means of livelihood. Unable to compete with the methods of cultivation used by the larger landowners, they were obliged to relinquish the few acres handed down to them: these now

> fall into the hands of wealthy purchasers, who . . . unite and consolidate; and, if they wish to become residents, erect new mansions out of the ruins of the ancient cottages, whose little enclosures, with all the wild graces that grew out of them, disappear . . .[1]

Those 'ancient cottages' of which Wordsworth was so fond, may Those 'ancient cottages' of which Wordsworth was so fond, may not have been commodious; yet they seemed to spring naturally out of the soil on which they stood. But the 'improvements' introduced by outsiders—men for the most part indifferent to the decline of cottage industries which Wordsworth finds so deplorable—betokened nothing but a lapse of taste, since the newcomers were concerned to see that their 'puny efforts of elegance' should predominate over the unpretentious dwellings which, for all their deficiencies, consorted well with the *genius loci*. Wordsworth's complaints about pompous artificiality, ornamental gardening and 'the craving for prospects' could be dwelt on at length; they are echoed in George Sturt's diatribes against the 'villa people' who come into Farnham and other places within easy reach of London and try to superimpose their commonplace mentality on the sounder old-fashioned taste of countrymen who have lived amid nature for long periods. The tone of resentment which appears in Sturt's remarks about 'resident trippers' (*Journals*,

[1] *Prose Works of William Wordsworth*, edited by William Knight (1896), II. 83.

20 May 1914) is foreshadowed in Wordsworth's comments on the disfigurement of Grasmere and district by 'new settlers' more interested in vulgar ostentation than in natural beauty.

Like Sturt, Wordsworth was actutely aware that the advantages arising from innovation for its own sake may be purchased at too great a cost. This is not the place to examine his views on the unsightliness of larch plantations and similar matters. Of more relevance are his remarks about the kind of life enjoyed by the 'poor laborious native' in the Lakeland area. More than once George Sturt has been adversely criticized for asking us to believe that 'In the Peasant times, whenever they were . . . it was enough for men to live in the folk way, fulfilling the traditions of their community, or of their caste . . .' (*Journals*, 26 August 1912); Sturt's confidence in the reality of the 'never-never land of the organic society'[1] is taken as evidence of simple-mindedness and feeble judgment. In view of this, it is interesting to find Wordsworth writing of 'a perfect Republic of Shepherds and Agriculturists' dwelling until recent times (sixty years ago) towards the head of the dales,

> among whom the plough of each man was confined to the maintenance of his own family, or to the occasional accomodation of his neighbour. . . . The chapel was the only edifice that presided over these dwellings, the supreme head of this pure Commonwealth; the members of which existed in the midst of a powerful empire, like an ideal society or an organized community, whose constitution had been imposed and regulated by the mountains which protected it . . .[2]

Admittedly, the Lake District is not Surrey or Hampshire, and Wordsworth may here be imposing on us ideas drawn from other countries. Nevertheless, he was prepared (like Sturt) to hazard the proposition that the 'social inheritance' of the peasant was one out of which responsible moral feelings might grow.[3] The era and

[1] See Graham Hough, 'Crisis in Literary Education' in ed. J. H. Plumb, *Crisis in the Humanities* (Pelican Books, 1964), p. 96.

[2] *Prose Works of William Wordsworth* ed. cit., II, 62–3.

[3] Cf. 'The Convention of Cintra' in *Prose Works of William Wordsworth* ed. cit., I. 256.

the conditions recalled by Wordsworth are not so very remote
from those remembered by Sturt's uncle John and his aunt Ann
Smith. Wordsworth writes:

> About the same time that strangers began to be attracted to
> the country, and to feel a desire to settle in it, the difficulty,
> that would have stood in the way of their procuring situations,
> was lessened by an unfortunate alteration in the circumstances
> of the native peasantry, proceeding from a cause which then
> began to operate, and is now felt in every house . . .[1]

He refers to the gradual diminution in extent of the cottage industries (a phenomenon which made the invention of machinery of
little real advantage to country people). Weaving, spinning and
other such activities were an essential part of the family life which
Wordsworth describes and which, as George Sturt suggested,
must have prevailed in most rural districts up to the time of
large-scale enclosures.[2] Of particular relevance to Sturt's own presentation of 'cottar' existence (as exemplified in his account of
an incident reported in the *Journals* for 25 December 1897) is a
footnote containing Wordsworth's comments on the manner
in which in the secluded and thinly populated areas of the Lake
District 'human happiness and comfort are dependent on the
contingency of neighbourhood . . .' 'This mutual helpfulness,'
he says,

> is not confined to out-of-doors work; but is ready upon all
> occasions. Formerly, if a person became sick, especially the
> mistress of a family, it was usual for those of the neighbours
> who were more particularly connected with the party by
> amicable offices, to visit the house carrying a present; this
> practice, which is by no means obsolete, is called *owning* the
> family, and is regarded as a pledge of a disposition to be other-
> wise serviceable in a time of disability and distress.[3]

Sturt was struck by much the same thing among the country
people he knew: 'It is an influence in sympathy, flowing, living,

[1] *Prose Works of William Wordsworth*, ed cit., II. 82.
[2] This was a subject Sturt often discussed with his gardener, Frederick
Grover. See *Journals* for 1 June 1904.
[3] *Prose Works of William Wordsworth* ed. cit., II. 62–3.

between the members of a group, and bringing to each one a delight in life from all,' he wrote in his *Journals* for 18 August 1917. He always insisted that one of the healthiest virtues of authentic peasant culture was the natural evolution of a spontaneous form of 'mutual aid'—not imposed in accordance with the will of a 'reformer' but evoked by the simple exigencies of communal life itself.

III

What I have called 'the English humanitarian tradition'— following up a suggestion made by George Sturt himself—embraces many more authors than those mentioned above. But it may not be an exaggeration to say that Sturt is perhaps the last significant representative of it. His sustained interest in 'the living past' as a subject of serious literary discussion was not a matter of mere antiquarianism; it sprang essentially from a conviction that the commercial aspects of applied science were bringing about what Wordsworth had called 'a warping of the natural mind'.[1] Among those who imagine that the summit of human felicity has been reached when 'letters are carried twelve times a day from Islington to Camberwell, and from Camberwell to Islington, and if railway trains run to and fro between them every quarter of an hour'[2] Sturt's writings will never command much respect. Yet in many of his works he reveals a peculiarly English manner of responding to the natural environment. And though in certain ways he was at variance with some of those whose attitudes he shared—Gilbert White, Constable and the later Wordsworth were all politically conservative—it seems fair to range him along with them by virtue of his unforced veneration for those permanent elements in the inherited order which they likewise had thought worthy of celebration.

---

[1] *Prose Works by William Wordsworth*, ed. cit., II. 68.
[2] Matthew Arnold, 'My Countrymen', *Cornhill Magazine*, February 1866.